I0006789

Upgrading to Microsoft® Windows® 2000 Professional

Upgrading to Microsoft® Windows® 2000 Professional

A Migration Guide For Windows® 98 and Windows® NT Users

Jerry Lee Ford, Jr.

Authors Choice Press

San Jose New York Lincoln Shanghai

Upgrading to Microsoft® Windows® 2000 Professional
A Migration Guide For Windows® 98 and Windows® NT Users

All Rights Reserved © 2000 by Jerry Lee Ford, Jr

No part of this book may be reproduced or transmitted in any form or by any means, graphic, electronic, or mechanical, including photocopying, recording, taping, or by any information storage or retrieval system, without the permission in writing from the publisher.

Authors Choice Press
an imprint of iUniverse.com, Inc.

For information address:
iUniverse.com, Inc.
5220 S 16th, Ste. 200
Lincoln, NE 68512
www.iuniverse.com

Microsoft and Microsoft Windows are trademarks of Microsoft Corporation. Every effort has been made to ensure the information presented in this book is accurate and reliable. This book is distributed and sold as is without warranty. The author is not responsible or liable for any problems or damages that may occur.

ISBN: 0-595-14804-2

Printed in the United States of America

To Mary, Alexander and William.

Contents

List of Tables

Acknowledgements

I would like to thank my mother, Martha Ford, for lending me her considerable talents and proofreading skills on yet another project.

Introduction

Upgrading to Windows 2000 is designed to assist people who are in the process of migrating from either Windows 98 or Windows NT Workstation 4 to Windows 2000 Professional and to help make that transition as smooth as possible. This book will also be beneficial for Windows 95 users since that operating is so similar to Windows 98.

Windows 2000 Professional is by far Microsoft's most advanced operating system. Its core is Windows NT. In fact its name was originally intended to be Windows NT Workstation 5. However, Microsoft changed the name to reflect the new operating system's appeal to a larger audience than just users in need of a powerful workstation. Microsoft even added the "Based on NT Technology" phrase to Windows 2000 Pro's startup splash screen to make sure that we do not forget its NT roots.

But while the heart of the operating system may be based on Windows NT, many of its new features are borrowed from Windows 98. In fact, the overall look and feel of Windows 2000 Professional is visually much more similar to Windows 98 than to Windows NT. The list below provides a comparison of the three Windows operating systems and their intended users.

- **Windows 98.** The home user with an emphasis on providing functionality for legacy software and hardware

- **Windows NT Workstation 4.** The corporate user and individuals requiring high end workstations with an emphasis on security at the sacrifice of some legacy software and hardware compatibility

- **Windows 2000 Professional.** The corporate user, individuals requiring high end workstations and home users with improved support for legacy hardware and software

Readership For This Book

Upgrading to Windows 2000 Professional is a quick reference guide for anyone who is currently using Windows 98 or Windows NT Workstation and needs to start working with Windows 2000 Professional. There are many new things you will need to learn about this new operating system. This book will help shorten your learning curve and serve as a guide for new features and the location of familiar tools in unfamiliar places.

Conventions Used in This Book

In order to make Upgrading to Windows 2000 Professional easer to read and understand, the following conventions have been used.

- **Bold.** Used to point out where you will need to provide information, click on an option or to place extra emphasize on certain text.

- <u>Underlined</u>. Use to identify keyboard shortcuts on menus and dialog boxes

In addition to the above conventions, this book makes liberal use of two other techniques for directing subject matter to your attention as outlined below:

NOTE: *Used to provide additional information or further insight on a topic.*

TIP!   *Used to provide information that, while not necessarily essential to the topic, offers advice that can help you save time or get additional benefit from a Windows 2000 feature.*

Chapter 1

New Features and Options in Windows 2000 Professional

Getting to Know Windows 2000 Professional

Microsoft Windows 2000 Professional is Microsoft's newest and most powerful desktop operating system. Originally named Windows NT Workstation 5, it was renamed to reflect Microsoft's intent that this operating system is designed for a broader audience. Windows 2000 Professional delivers an impressive list of new features and functionality that work together to deliver an operating system that is easier to use than Windows 98 and yet more secure and reliable than Windows NT Workstation 4.

1

Easy to use

Microsoft has added an impressive array of new features to Windows 2000 Professional that make it the most user-friendly operating system available. The following list describes many of these new features:

- **Improved Performance.** Windows 98 users should see a 25 percent faster performance increase on systems with at least 64 MB of memory.

- **Intelligent Desktop Menus.** The operating system constantly monitors how users use their computer and adapts by organizing menus to present the applications that are most often accessed.

- **New Wizards.** Microsoft has added many new wizards that streamline both routine and advanced system configuration changes such as printer installation or modem sharing.

- **New Troubleshooters.** Microsoft has added new troubleshooters that allow users to solve many typical problems without requiring expert assistance.

- **Histories.** Just about every Windows dialog now maintains a list of local files and folders, network resources and even web sites that users have accessed making it easy for users to access them again.

- **Hibernation.** Allows users to turn off their computer while saving their current settings and applications and restores them to their previous state when the computer is restarted.

- **Mobile Computing.** Built-in support for technologies such as plug and play, hot docking, advanced power management and USB makes Windows 2000 Professional the best notebook operating system ever.

Microsoft has borrowed many of Windows 2000 Professional's new features from Windows 98 as demonstrated in the following list:

- **AutoComplete.** The operating system tracks users as they work and will complete URL addresses as users begin to type them.

- **AutoCorrect.** Windows will automatically recognize and fix typos in URL address syntax.

- **Plug and Play.** The addition of advanced plug and play functionality provides for trouble free installation of new hardware.

- **Expanded Hardware Support.** Windows 2000 supports the latest advances in hardware technology including support for the Universal Serial Bus (USB), IEEE 1394 (Fire Wire), DVD drives, and the Accelerated Graphics Port (AGP) video card.

- **Multiple Monitors.** Users can install multiple video cards allowing users to work with two or more monitors at a time.

- **Mobile Computing.** Microsoft has added many new improvements for the mobile user including support for hot docking and plug and play.

In addition to borrowing features from Windows 98, Microsoft has retained and improved upon many of the core technologies Windows NT Workstation 4 users may be familiar working with including:

- **Microsoft Management Consoles (MMC).** Microsoft has standardized Windows 2000 Professional administration by borrowing the MMC from Internet Information Server. Utilities that manage such things as performance monitoring, services and event logs now have a similar look and feel.

- **Indexing.** This is another feature borrowed from Internet Information Server. It allows the operating system to scan every file of the local system and build a comprehensive index which users can then search to more quickly locate files.

- **NTFS Version 5.** Building upon the strengths of Windows NT Workstations 4's NTFS, Microsoft has updated the file system to include support for encrypting data stored on local hard drives.

More Secure and Reliable

Windows 98 is an operating system designed to provide ease of use and support for a wide range of software and hardware. Windows NT Workstation 4 was designed to provide reliable performance and high security. Often Windows NT provided these features at the loss of support for many legacy hardware devices and older software programs. Windows 2000 addresses these issues and provides a range of new features designed to provide more compatibility with even higher levels of reliability and security. Among its new features are:

- **Windows NT Security Model.** Windows 2000 Professional supports Windows NT Workstation's security model while integrating better with networks that use Windows 2000 Active Directory.

- **Encrypted File System.** Windows 2000 allows users to selectively encrypt individual files, folders or entire disk drives to further secure important data.

- **Windows File Protection.** Windows tracks critical system files and can automatically restore them in the event that they are accidentally corrupted or deleted.

- **Driver Certification.** Microsoft provides device driver certificates that ensure software drivers have been quality tested.

- **Reduced Number of System Restarts.** Microsoft has reduced the number of scenarios that require the system be restarted from 75 to 7 thus allowing many types of system configuration changes to occur without disrupting system availability.

- **Advanced File System Support.** Windows 2000 Professional provides support for all major files systems including FAT, FAT32 and NTFS version 4 and NTFS version 5.

- **Safe Mode.** Windows 2000 now incorporates the Windows 98 Safe Mode, which allows users to start their systems in a various basic modes with a minimal set of device drivers.

NOTE: *Because Windows 2000 is so security conscious there are many things that a typical user cannot do even on their own computer unless they have been assigned administrative authority. A special user account, the administrator account, is created during the installation of Windows 2000. This is the most powerful account on the computer. It is a member of a group called the Administrators group. Unless you have access to the administrator account or have an account in the administrators group, you are going to be restricted as to what you can do on your computer. Windows NT has always worked this way, but this may come as a bit of a surprise to Windows 98 users.*

Easier Networking

Microsoft has simplified network configuration by adding a host of new tools to Windows 2000 Pro that guide you through the most complex networking tasks. These include:

- **Easier Peer to Peer Networking.** Windows 2000's plug and play and other networking features makes adding a Windows 2000 computer to a client/server network easy. It includes full support for peer networking with other Windows operating systems.

- **Network Connection Wizard.** This wizard steps users through the process of configuring Windows 2000 networking including the setup of features such as Internet access, PC to PC connections and modem sharing.

- **Automatic IP Address Allocation.** On small networks without a DHCP server Windows 2000 will automatically configure its own IP address allowing immediate network access without requiring the user to perform any complex configuration.

- **Integration with Internet Explorer 5.01.** Windows 2000 is fully integrated with Internet Explorer allowing users to access web sites and resources as easily as local network resources.

- **Modem Sharing.** Windows 2000 supports shared access to remote networks or to the Internet by allowing local modems to provide proxy services to other network computers.

- **Automatic Proxy Configuration.** Windows 2000 computers can automatically locate and configure themselves to use network shared modems.

Hardware Requirements

If Microsoft has its way, Windows 2000 Professional will become the desktop of choice in the business community. Microsoft also expects the product to attract many home users. This is one of the reasons why Microsoft has worked so hard to make the operating system look and behave so much like Windows 98. The good news is that this makes the operating system must easier for the user to operate. The bad news is that all this simplicity comes with a price. While the outside looks sleek and efficient, the inside is built around a very powerful and complex set of technologies. All this power means that Windows 2000 Professional has substantially higher resource requirements than either Windows 98 or Windows NT 4. In fact, while other Microsoft desktop operating systems will operate well with 16 MB of memory on a 486 or Pentium based system with a few hundred MB of disk space, Windows 2000 Pro requires substantially more resources as shown in Table 1.1.

Table 1.1 Comparison of Windows Operating System Minimum Requirements

	Memory	CPU	Hard disk
Windows 98	16 MB	80486	175
Windows NT Workstation 4	16 MB	80486	117
Windows 2000 Professional	64 MB	Pentium 133	650

Where has Everything Gone?

Perhaps the biggest challenge most Windows 98 and Windows NT users will face in working with Windows 2000 Professional is finding where familiar tools or equivalent tools are located in Windows 2000. Microsoft has changed the locations of many utilities and their new location is not always obvious. Tables 1.2 and 1.3 present a list of Windows 98 and Windows NT Workstation tools and the names and locations of corresponding tools in Windows 2000 Professional as well as the page number where the utility is covered in this book.

Table 1.2 Finding Equivalent Windows 98 Tools in Windows 2000 Professional

Windows 98 Feature	Windows 2000 Professional Location/Tool
Active Desktop	Start→ Settings→ Control Panel→ FolderOptions→ General Tab→ Active Desktop
Address Book	Start→ Programs→ Accessories→ Address Book
Clipboard Viewer	Start→ Run→ Type Clipbrd
Compression Agent	Start→ Programs→ Accessories→ Windows Explorer

Computer Name	Start→ Settings→ Control Panel→ System Network Identification tab→ Network ID
Connection Wizard	Start→ Settings→ Network and Dial-up→ Connections→ Make New Connection
Device Manager	Start→ Settings→ Control Panel→ System→ Hardware Tab→ Device Manager
Dial-Up Networking	Start→ Programs→ Accessories→ Communications→ Network and Dial-up Connections→ Make New Connection
Direct Cable Connection	Start→ Programs→ Accessories→ Communications→ Network and Dial-up Connections→ Make New Connection
Disconnect Network Drive	My Computer or My Network Places Menu
Drive Converter (Fat32)	Start→ Settings→ Control Panel→ Administrative Tools→ Computer Management→ Storage→ Disk Management
DriveSpace	Start→ Settings→ Control Panel→ Administrative Tools→ Computer Management→ Storage→ Disk Management
Find	Start→ Search
Folder Options	Start→ Settings→ Control Panel→ Folder Options
Internet Explorer 4	Start→ Programs→ Internet Explorer
Log Off	Start→ Settings→ Taskbar & Start Menu→ Advanced Tab→ Start Menu Settings→ Display Logoff
Map Network Drive	My Computer or My Network Places Menu
MD-DOS Prompt	Start→ Programs→ Accessories→ Command Prompt

Media Player	Start→ Programs→ Accessories→ Entertainment→ Windows Media Player
My Briefcase	Start→ Programs→ Accessories→ Synchronize
Multimedia Applet	Start→ Settings→ Control Panel→ Sounds and Multimedia
NetMeeting	Start→ Programs→ Accessories→ Communicationsn NetMeeting
Net Watcher	Start→ Settings→ Control Panel→ Administrative Tools→ Computer Management→ Shared Folders
Network Dialog	Start→ Settings→ Network and Dial-up Connections→ Local Area Connection→ Properties
Network Identification	Start→ Settings→ Control Panel→ System→ Network Identification Tab→ Properties
Network Neighborhood	My Network Places
Outlook Express 4	Start→ Programs→ Outlook Express
Passwords	Ctrl+Alt+Del→ Change Password
Power Management	Start→ Settings→ Control Panel→ Power Options
Resource Meter	Ctrl+Alt+Del→ Task Manager
ScanDisk	My Computer→ Select a local Disk→ File Menu→ Properties→ Tools Tab→ Error-checking→ Check Now
Sounds	Start→ Settings→ Control Panel→ Sounds and Multimedia
System Monitor	Start→ Settings→ Control Panel→ Administrative Tools→ Performance

Telnet Client	Start→ Run→ Telnet
Users Applet	Start→ Settings→ Control Panel→ Users and Passwords or Start→ Settings→ Control Panel→ Administrative Tools→ Computer Management→ Local Users and Groups
Welcome To Windows	Start→ Programs→ Accessories→ System Tools→ Getting Started
Windows Explorer	Start→ Programs→ Accessories→ Windows Explorer

Table 1.3 Finding Equivalent Windows NT Workstation 4 Tools in Windows 2000 Professional

Windows NT Feature	Windows 2000 Professional Location/Tool
Backup	Start→ Programs→ Accessories→ System Tools→ Backup
Command Prompt	Start→ Programs→ Accessories→ Command Prompt
Computer Identification	Start→ Settings→ Control Panel→ System→ Network Identification Tab→ Network ID
Devices Applet	Start→ Settings→ Control Panel→ Administrative Tools→ Computer Management→ Device Manager
Dial-up Networking	Start→ Settings→ Network and Dial-up Connections
Direct Cable Connection	Start→ Settings→ Network and Dial-up Connections
Disconnect Network	Drive My Computer or My Network Places Menu
Disk Administrator	Start→ Settings→ Control Panel→ Administrative Tools→ Computer Management→ Storage→ Disk Management
Event Viewer	Start→ Settings→ Control Panel→ Administrative Tools→ Computer Management→ System Tools→ Event Viewer

Find	Start→ Search
HyperTerminal	Start→ Programs→ Accessories→ Communications→ HyperTerminal
Inbox	Start→ Programs→ Outlook Express
Internet Explorer 2	Start→ Programs→ Internet Explorer
Network Neighborhood	My Network Places
Map Network Drive	My Computer or My Network Places Menu
Multimedia Applet	Start→ Settings→ Control Panel→ Sounds and Multimedia
My Briefcase	Start→ Programs→ Accessories→ Synchronize
Network Dialog	Start→ Settings→ Network and Dial-up Connections→ Local Area Connection→ Properties
Network Identification	Start→ Settings→ Control Panel→ System→ Network Identification Tab→ roperties
ODBC	Start→ Settings→ Control Panel→ Administrative Tools→ Data Source (ODBC)
Performance Monitor	Start→ Settings→ Control Panel→ Administrative Tools→ Performance
Phone Dialer	Start→ Programs→ Accessories→ Communications→ Phone Dialer
Ports	Start→ Settings→ Control Panel→ Administrative Tools→ Computer Management→ Device Manager
SCSI Adapters Applet	Start→ Settings→ Control Panel→ Administrative Tools→ Computer Management→ Device Manager

Server Applet	Start→ Settings→ Control Panel→ Administrative Tools→ Computer Management→ Shared Folders
Services Applet	Start→ Settings→ Control Panel→ Administrative Tools→ Services
Tape Devices	Start→ Settings→ Control Panel→ Administrative Tools→ Computer Management→ Device Manager
Telnet Client	Start→ Run→ Telnet
User Manager	Start→ Settings→ Control Panel→ Users and Passwords or Start→ Settings→ Control Panel→ Administrative Tools→ Computer Management→ Local Users and Groups
Windows Explorer	Start→ Programs→ Accessories→ Windows Explorer
Windows NT Diagnostics	Start→ Programs→ Accessories→ System Tools→ System Information

Chapter 2

Getting Started

Getting Ready to Upgrade to Windows 2000 Professional

Upgrading your operating system from Windows 98 or Windows NT Workstation 4 to Windows 2000 Professional is a snap as long as you do your homework first. This includes reviewing the installation process and ensuring that your hardware and software is Windows 2000 compatible. Once you have things up and running, you will find Windows 2000 Professional is every bit as easy to work with as Windows 98 and as powerful as Windows NT.

Migration Paths from Windows 95, 98 and NT

If your computer has adequate hardware to support Windows 2000 Professional, it will always benefit you to upgrade from Windows NT Workstation 4 because of its improved hardware support, better user interface and superior performance. The benefit of upgrading from Windows 98 to Windows 2000 Professional depends on several factors including:

- **Does the computer have adequate hardware resources.** If not you should upgrade your hardware or remain with Windows 98

- **Does Windows 2000 Professional support all your software.** Check the web sites of the software vendors who created your applications. If a key application is not supported on Windows 2000 Professional you may need to either stay with Windows 98 or switch to another vendor's application.

- **Is your current hardware on the Windows 2000 Hardware Compatibility List or HCL?** As of the writing of this book Microsoft keeps an updated copy of the HCL at http://www.microsoft.com/hwtest.hcl. If your hardware is not listed you may need to either purchase replacement hardware or stay with Windows 98.

The following table compares several key differences between Windows 98, Windows NT and Windows 2000 to help you decide if upgrading to Windows 2000 is appropriate for your situation.

Table 2.1 Operating System Comparison

Operating System Support For:	Windows 98	Windows NT Workstation 4	Windows 2000 Professional
Support for latest hardware devices	YES	NO	YES
NTFS 5	NO	With SP4	YES
FAT32	Yes	NO	YES
FAT	YES	YES	YES
Plug and Play	YES	NO	YES
Legacy software	YES	Partial	Improved
Legacy hardware	YES	Limited	Improved

Windows 98 and Windows NT Workstation 4 are not the only Microsoft operating systems that can be upgraded to Windows 2000 Professional. Windows NT Workstation 4 is the best upgrade path. As Windows 2000's direct predecessor, Windows NT is the most similar operating system, and it shares a similar registry database. Upgrading from the other operating systems will probably mean a loss of some customization and may even require some of your applications be reinstalled. The list of operating systems that can be upgraded includes:

- MS-DOS

- Windows 3.1

- Windows 95

- Windows 98

- Windows NT 3.51

- Windows NT 4

Regardless of which operating system you are upgrading from, Windows 2000 Professional provides you with two options. The first option allows you to upgrade your current operating system thus migrating almost all of your current customization. The second option allows you to install a new copy of Windows 2000 giving you a fresh start but requiring you to reinstall all your applications and redo all your customization.

File System Support (FAT, FAT32, NTFS)

One major decision you must make when upgrading to Windows 2000 is what file system to use. Windows 2000 Professional still supports the same file systems as Windows NT Workstation 4.0, namely FAT and NTFS version 4. Microsoft has also added support for FAT32 which was introduced by Windows 95 Release 2 and Windows 98. In addition it introduces NTFS version 5, the most secure and reliable file system to date.

FAT32 is a 32-bit version of FAT that provides more efficient use of space, allowing for as much as 30 percent more storage on the same drive. FAT32, however, is not a secure operating system. NTFS is a very secure file system. It provides the establishment of security permissions. This allows access to files and folders to be secured on an individual or group basis. The following table compares Windows 2000 Professional's file system support with that of other Microsoft operating systems.

Table 2.2 File Systems Supported By Microsoft Operating Systems

	Windows 95	Windows 98	Windows NT	Windows 2000
FAT	Yes	Yes	Yes	Yes
FAT32	OSR2 only	Yes	No	Yes
NTFS 4	No	No	Yes	Yes
NTFS 5	No	No	Partial with SP4	Yes

NTFS version 5 provides Windows 2000 Professional with several new features. These include:

- **Data encryption.** The ability to encrypt files, folders or an entire disk drive.

- **Disk quotas.** The ability to set predefined limits on the amount of storage space that a user or group of users can use on a specified hard drive.

- **Disk indexing.** Allows the operating system to examine the contents of files stored on a given disk drive as well as each file's properties in order to create a searchable index.

NOTE: *While disks drives formatted with a FAT file system can be converted to NTFS, NTFS formatted volumes cannot be converted to FAT.*

Upgrade Packs

Some of your applications that worked well on Windows 98 or Windows NT may not work on Windows 2000 Professional. In many cases the vendor who created the application will provide an upgrade pack for the application. An upgrade pack is a set of programs and files Windows uses to upgrade the application so that it will work on Windows 2000.

Most applications are going to work perfectly fine on Windows 2000 Professional. If after visiting the web sites of your application's vendors you discover that you have an incompatible application and that no upgrade pack has been created for it, you will need to either remain on your current operating system until a upgrade pack is made available or switch to a replacement application that is compatible with Windows 2000.

You can run the Windows 2000 setup program winnt32.exe with the */checkupgradeonly* option to create an upgrade report for your computer without actually upgrading to Windows 2000. This report will provide a list of applications that require upgrade packs. However, there is no guarantee that the report will be able to identify every application that may require an upgrade pack.

TIP! *Make sure you have downloaded any required upgrade packs before starting the upgrade to Windows 2000 to ensure the smoothest transition when converting to Windows 2000 Professional*

Upgrading to Windows 2000 Professional

Upgrading from Windows 98 or Windows NT Workstation to Windows 2000 Professional involves the same basic set of steps with only a few minor differences. On MS-DOS and Windows 3.1 operating systems you must run the Winnt.exe program. This is a 16-bit version of the Windows 2000 setup program. If you are upgrading from Windows 95, Windows 98 or Windows NT, run the Winnt32.exe program. This is the 32-bit version of the Windows 2000 setup program. Because all Windows NT and Windows 2000 computers that are members of a Windows domain require computer accounts, you will need to make sure that your network administrator has created one for your computer if you are upgrading to Windows 2000 from any other operating system than Windows NT. Loading the Windows 2000 Professional CD-ROM should automatically start the Winnt32.exe program on Windows 95, Windows 98 and Windows NT computers. If not you can find it on your Windows 2000 CD-ROM at \i386\winnt32.exe.

There are too many possible combinations of steps to cover each in detail when upgrading from Windows 98 or Windows NT. The basic steps for upgrading your current operating system to Windows 2000 Professional are outlined below:

1. Turn on your computer and allow the current operating system to start.

2. Make a backup copy of all your important files and data just in case something goes wrong.

3. Insert the Windows 2000 Professional CD-ROM. A prompt appears asking if you would like to upgrade to Windows 2000. Click on **Yes**.

4. When prompted select **Upgrade to Windows 2000** and click on **Next**.

5. You are presented with the Windows 2000 License Agreement. Select **I accept this agreement** and click on **Next**.

6. A dialog appears advising you that you should visit the Windows Compatibility Web site before performing the upgrade. Click on **Next** to continue.

7. Some Windows applications require upgrade packs in order to operate properly on Windows 2000. If you do not have any upgrade packs or are not sure select **No, I don't have any upgrade packs** and click on **Next**. Setup will also create a report informing you if it identified the need for any upgrade packs which you can the apply at a later date.

8. If you are upgrading from any Microsoft operating system other than Windows NT, you are prompted to upgrade your file system to

NTFS. Unless you plan to run more than one operating system at a time on your computer, you should select <u>Y</u>es, **upgrade my drive** and click on <u>N</u>ext.

9. The setup process begins analyzing you computer and produces an upgrade report summarizing any compatibility issues that it may have found. As long as there are no major problems reported, click on <u>N</u>ext.

10. Setup announces that it is ready to perform the installation and that it will start copying files to your computer, convert it file system to NTFS if that option was selected and reboot the computer multiple times. Click on <u>N</u>ext to begin the install.

11. During the next 30 minutes to an hour, setup will detect your hard disks, copy files to your hard drive, initialize Windows 2000 and convert the file system to NTFS if required.

12. Next Windows 2000 will detect and install devices that it discovers on your computer. If it detects a network interface card or NIC, Windows 2000 will then configure the computer for networking. If the previous operating system was already configured for networking, Windows 2000 will migrate its settings.

13. Next Windows 2000 installs various system components required for normal operations.

14. Windows 2000 Professional announces that it is completing its final installation tasks. These include installing Start menu items, registering components, upgrading programs and system settings, saving settings and removing any temporary files that were used.

15. You are presented with the Log On to Windows dialog allowing you to log onto Windows 2000 Professional.

NOTE: *During the installation of Windows 2000 three user accounts are created: Administrator, Guest and a user account. In addition, Windows 2000 will migrate user and group accounts from the previous operating system. Because the Administrator account is very powerful, it is strongly recommended that you use the normal user account for your daily work. If necessary you can add administrative privileges to your normal user account into a special administrators group using the Users and Passwords utility. For more information on Windows 2000 security, see "Managing User and Group Accounts" at the end of this chapter.*

Working With Windows 2000 Professional for the First Time

There are a few things you need to know before you start using your new operating system. If you are a Windows NT user you should already be somewhat familiar with basic tasks such as logging on and off and locking your system. But if you are upgrading from Windows 98 you need to get used to these new tasks.

Logging In

Windows 2000 Professional employs user accounts and passwords to identify and authenticate users in the same manner as Windows NT Workstation. Users must present their logon name and password credentials in order to complete a successful login. This differs from Windows 98 where a user without valid credentials can press Cancel at the login prompt and still gain access to the local computer and its resources.

If your computer is part of a windows domain network, authentication will be performed by a network computer known as a domain controller. If your computer is on a peer network or running as a stand-alone device, you will be authenticated locally.

Normally every person who logs onto the computer requires a unique user name and an associated password. The Windows 2000 Professional logon process allows you to supply the computer with this information.

NOTE: *You can set up you computer to bypass the login process when it is started. This procedure is described later in this chapter in the section titled "Establishing a Non-authenticated login".*

When Windows 2000 Professional starts, it displays the Welcome to Windows screen. In order to initiate a login you must press and hold CTRL+ALT+DEL. This unique key sequence is designed to halt all other active programs during the login process in order to prevent any trojan horse programs from trying to imitate the login process and steal user names and passwords.

After typing your user name and password, Windows 2000 will try to authenticate your account information. It does this by searching the local security database to find a matching user account and password or by requesting a domain controller perform authentication. If you do not have an account or have mistyped either your user name or password, your logon is rejected and access is denied. If successful, Windows will create an access token for you and complete your login.

Welcome to Windows 2000

The first thing you will see after logging on to Windows 2000 Professional is the Getting Started with Windows 2000 dialog as shown in Figure 2.1. It provides the following options:

- **Register Now.** Assists you in registering your copy of Windows 2000 Professional with Microsoft.

- **Discover Windows.** Provides an overview of new Windows 2000 features.

- **Connect to the Internet.** Starts the Internet Connection Wizard, which will guide you through the process of establishing Internet access.

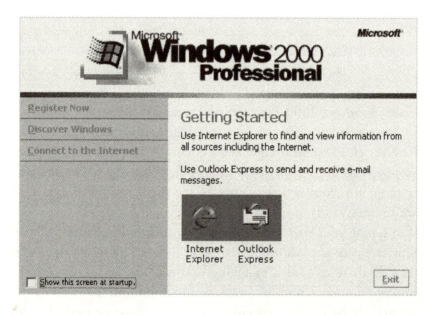

Figure 2.1 The Getting Started with Windows 2000 Dialog

Deselecting the Show this screen at startup option at the bottom left corner of the dialog prevents this dialog from appearing the next time you log on. If you wish to revisit it later you may do so by selecting Start, Programs, Accessories, System Tools and then Getting Started.

The Welcome to Windows 2000 dialog is almost identical to the Welcome to Windows 98 dialog that appears the first time you log onto a Windows 98 computer. The Welcome to Windows 98 dialog includes a fourth option called Maintain Your Computer which when selected starts the Windows 98 Maintenance wizard. This wizard allows you to establish a maintenance schedule for defragmenting your local hard disks, scanning local disk drives for errors and deleting unnecessary files for disk drives. Similar functionality is provided in Windows 2000 Professional using the Scheduled Task Wizard, which is started by selecting Start, Programs, Accessories, System Tools, Schedules Tasks and then double-clicking on the Add Scheduled Task icon.

The Welcome Dialog on Windows NT also appears when you first log on to Windows NT Workstation. Like Windows 98 and Windows 2000 it has an option to prevent it from appearing the next time you logon. This dialog provides a unique instruction tip every time it is run. In addition, it provides an overview of changes from Windows NT 3.5.1 and easy access to the Windows NT help system.

Changing Your Password

Changing your password regularly helps protect your computer and network. Usually your network administrator will establish a policy that forces you to change your password at regular intervals. In addition, your administrator may establish policies that govern the minimum length and composition of passwords. Even if your network does not have such a policy it is a good idea to change your password often, especially if you suspect that it has somehow been compromised.

You can change your password in Windows 98 by double-clicking on the Passwords icon in the Windows 98 Control Panel. This opens the Passwords properties dialog where you can select the Change Windows Password button and then change your password.

Windows NT Workstation 4 and Windows 2000 Professional both handle password changing in the same manner. First you must press the CTRL+ALT+DEL key sequence. This starts the Windows Security dialog as shown in Figure 2.2. From here you select the Change Password option to open the Change Password dialog as shown in Figure 2.3. To change your password type your old password and then your new password twice before clicking on OK.

Figures 2.2 and 2.3 Show the Windows Security and Change Password Dialogs

NOTE: *You can also change your password by clicking on the Set Password button on the Users property sheet of Users and Passwords utility. If you are a member of the administrators* *group, you can reset passwords for other users who share the computer.*

TIP! *Windows 98 only supports passwords up to 14 characters in length. If you will be logging in to a network from Windows 98 computers as well as your Windows 2000 Professional system, limit your password to 14 or less characters. Otherwise, you will not be able to log into the network from any Windows 98 computers.*

Logging Off

Whenever you are finished working with Windows 2000 Professional is always best to log off. This protects your system from being accessed by someone should you step away for a while.

To log off a Windows 98 computer you select Start and then Log Off and click on Yes when prompted to confirm your log off. To log off a Windows NT computer you can either select Start, Shut Down, Close all programs and log on as a different user, and click on Yes or you can press CTRL+ALT+DEL and select Logoff from the Security dialog and then click on OK when prompted for confirmation.

Windows 2000 Professional provides the same two options for logging off as Windows NT and adds the ability to configure a Log off option on the Start menu. To enable this option select Start, Settings, Taskbar, select the Advance tab and then select Display Logoff and click on OK as shown in Figure 2.4. The Log Off options now appears on the Start menu as shown in Figure 2.5.

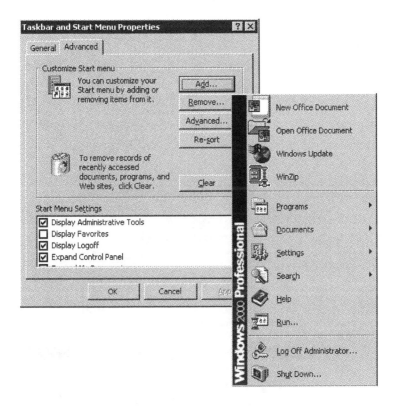

*Figures 2.4 and 2.5 Demonstrate How to Add a Logoff Option
to the Windows 2000 Start Menu*

Locking Windows 2000

On Windows 98 you can either log off of your computer or shut it down when you are not using it. Windows NT and Windows 2000 provide the option of locking your computer when you only need to leave it for a few moments. This prevents you from having to close all your open applications and log off or shut down just so you can return in log on and open them again.

To lock you computer press CTRL+ALT+DEL and select Lock Computer on the Windows Security dialog. The Computer Locked dialog appears as shown in Figure 2.6. Only you or a member of the administrators group can unlock the computer. To unlock it press CTRL+ALT+DEL, type your password and click on OK as shown in Figure 2.7.

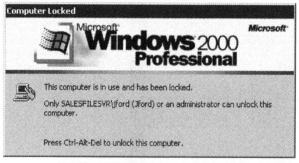

Figures 2.6 and 2.7 Demonstrate How to Unlock a Windows 2000 Computer

Another way to lock your computer is by using a password protected screen saver that automatically starts after a specified period of time has passed during which you have not used your computer. Windows 98, Windows NT and Windows 2000 all provide this capability. However, the purpose of locking a Windows 98 computer with a password protected screen saver can be defeated by powering down the computer, starting it and pressing Cancel at the logon prompt.

Shutdown Options

The shutdown process for Windows 2000 Professional is very similar to that of Windows 98 and Windows NT. All three operating systems provide the option to shut down or shut down and restart the computer by clicking on Start, Shut Down and then selecting either the shutdown or restart option and confirming your selection. All three operating systems also provide the option of initiating a shutdown by pressing CTRL+ALT+DEL and then selecting Shut Down. Windows 2000 and Windows NT also provide a Restart option for this method.

In addition to the above shutdown options, Windows 98 and Windows 2000 provide two other options, which are part of their new power management feature. These options are:

- **Stand by.** Places a copy of all running programs and data in memory and reduces the power supply to certain hardware components such as the monitor and disk drive. When you return and move the mouse or click on the keyboard, Windows 2000 restores normal power and returns your desktop to its previous state.

- **Hibernate.** Places a copy of all running programs and data on the hard disk and powers down the computer. When you return and power the computer back on, Windows 2000 loads quickly and returns your desktop to its previous state.

Typically you use standby if you are only going to be away from your computer for a short time and hibernate for longer periods of time.

TIP!   *Consider using Standby as a means of conserving power and extending the life of your battery when working on a laptop computer.*

Establishing a Non-authenticated Login

A new feature introduced by Windows 2000 Professional is the ability to configure your computer so that it automatically logs on using a predefined user name and password. This does not eliminate the requirement for a user name and password. It simply automates the login process. This is distinctly different from bypassing the login process on Windows 98 by clicking on Cancel at the logon prompt.

Automatic login is configured using the Network Identification Wizard as follows:

1. Double-click on the System icon in the Windows 2000 Control Panel to open the System Properties dialog.

2. Select the Network Identification property sheet and click on **Network ID** to start the Network Identification Wizard. Click on **Next**.

3. Select **This computer is for home use and is not part of a business network** and click on **Next**.

4. Select **Windows always assumes the following user has logged on to this computer** and provide the required user name and password information as shown in Figure 2.8. Click on **Next** and then **Finish**.

5. Click on **OK** when notified that the computer will need to be restarted in order for your changes to take effect.

6. Click on **Yes** to restart the computer.

After the computer restarts, it automatically logs on using the user name and password that you provided. If you open the Users and Passwords utility from the Windows 2000 Control Panel you will see that the Users must <u>e</u>nter a user name and password to use this computer option has been disabled as shown in Figure 2.8. Selecting this option restores the requirement that users provide their user name and password credentials before accessing the computer. You could also restore this requirement by rerunning the Network Identification Wizard.

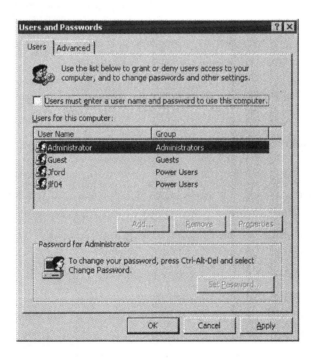

Figure 2.8 Viewing the Login Requirement

NOTE: *This is a very dangerous option because it allows anyone with physical access to the computer to login. If the computer is attached to a network it, allows access to the network as well. This may be desirable for a home computer, but you should consult with your network administrator before trying to configure this option at work.*

Installing New Hardware

With the addition of plug and play support, Windows 2000 Professional leaves behind a legacy of hardware compatibility and configuration issues that has plagued Windows NT since its introduction. This includes support for non-plug and play devices as well.

Plug and Play

Plug and play hardware is a new generation of computer hardware designed so that it can be automatically detected and configured by the operating system. Windows 2000 Professional and Windows 98 both provide advanced plug and play support. Windows NT Workstation does not provide this feature.

Installing plug and play hardware is very easy. Simply install the device and turn your computer on. Windows 2000 Professional should automatically discover the new device and configure it. The one exception is Windows 2000 might need to prompt you for a device software driver if it does not already have one.

NOTE: *If Windows 2000 displays a Digital Signature Not Found dialog then the software driver that you supplied has not been tested by Microsoft. This does not mean that the driver will not work correctly. You may instruct Windows 2000 to use the driver anyway. Check the hardware vendor's web site to see if a Windows 2000 version of the software driver has been made available for download.*

Windows 2000 provides the Device Manager utility, shown in Figure 2.9, for viewing your hardware. You can check on the status of any peripheral device using this utility and make sure that the plug and play process successfully installed and configured your new hardware. Windows 98 also supplies a version of the Device Manager utility that provides that operating system with similar functionality.

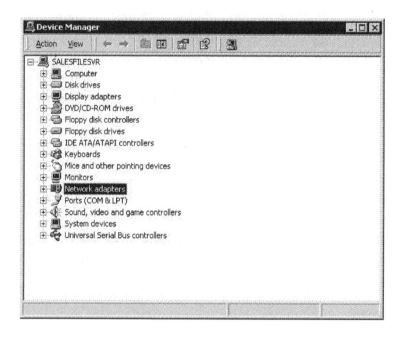

*Figure 2.9 The Windows 2000 Device Manger Can Be Used
to View the Status of Your Plug and Play Hardware*

Non-Plug and Play

Even if you have hardware that is not plug and play compatible
Windows 2000 may still be able to work with it if the manufacturer has
created a plug and play software driver for the device. This will allows
Windows 2000 to provide partial support.

If neither a device nor its driver is plug and play compatible,
Windows 2000 may still be able to work with it. However, Windows
2000 will not be able to provide any power management over it no will

it be able to automatically install it. Instead you must run the Add/Remove Hardware utility.

To install a non-plug and play device you need to run the Add/Remove Hardware Wizard using the following procedure:

1. Double-click on the Add/Remove hardware icon on the Windows 2000 Control Panel to start the Add/Remove Hardware Wizard and click on **N**ext.

2. Select **A**dd/**T**roubleshoot a device and click on **N**ext.

3. Windows 2000 will automatically scan for new plug and play hardware. When it fails to locate any new hardware it assumes that you want to troubleshoot an existing device. Select **Add a new device** and click on **N**ext.

4. Select **N**o**, I want to select the hardware from a list** and click on **N**ext.

5. Select the type of hardware you are installing and click on **N**ext.

6. What happens next depends upon the type of device that you are installing. Continue to follow the instructions presented. You may be required to provide a software driver. When prompted click on **F**inish.

Installing New Software

Windows 2000 has streamlined the software installation process while at the same time making your applications easier to manage. Application installation, configuration, repair and removal are quietly managed behind the scenes guaranteeing a more stable and reliable working environment.

Add/Remove Programs

Windows 98 and Windows NT provide the Add/Remove Programs utility as a tool for adding, viewing and removing applications and Windows components. The Windows 98 Add/Remove Programs utility also allows you to create a Startup disk containing important system configuration information and files, which you can use to help repair your Windows 98 computer when certain problems arise.

Windows 2000 Professional has made significant changes to the Add/Remove Programs utility. However, it does not provide the option of creating a repair disk. This feature is now located in the Windows 2000 Backup utility.

The Windows 2000 Add/Remove Programs utility integrates with the Windows Installer Service. This is a new Windows service that is designed to manage the installation and removal of applications and Windows components. Applications designed to work with this service register their files and registry entries so that this service can monitor and track them. If something should happen to these files or registry entries, Windows 2000 Professional can automatically restore them. When you use the Add/Remove Programs utility to remove an application, the Windows Installer Service ensures that every file, shortcut and registry entry for the application is removed. This helps to ensure a cleaner and more reliable system.

The Windows 2000 Add/Remove Programs dialog is shown in Figure 2.10. It is started by double-clicking on the Add/Remove Programs icon on the Windows 2000 Control Panel. The features provided by this utility are organized into three categories and are started by clicking on their icons on the left pane of the dialog. These categories are:

- **Change or Remove Programs.** Displays all currently installed applications and allows you to modify or uninstall them.

- **Add New Programs.** Allows you to install your applications such as Microsoft Office.

- **Add/Remove Windows Components.** Allows you to install and uninstall Windows 2000 components which you did not install during the initial installation of Windows 2000 Professional.

The Add/Remove Programs dialog now supports network installations and allows you to sort the display based on any of the following options:

- Name

- Size

- Frequency Of Use

- Time Last Used

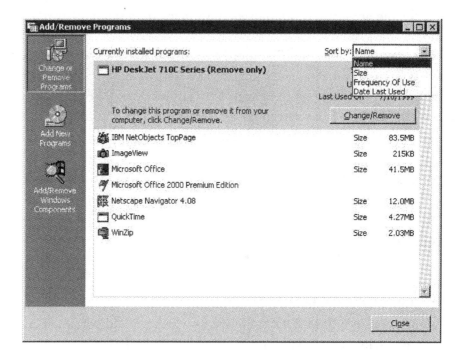

Figure 2.10 The Add/Remove Programs Utility

Change or Remove Programs

The first option on the Add/Remove Programs utility displays a list of currently installed programs and provides additional information not found in Windows 98 or Windows NT including the amount of hard drive space used by each program, how often applications are used and the date it was last used. The Change and Remove options allow you to modify the current application's installation or to remove it from your computer.

When a particular application is selected, Windows displays a support information option, if it is available, that provides access to information such as vendor name, version number and vendor support web site address. In addition to vendor and application information, you may also find an option to run a repair process in the event that any key files used by the program have been damaged or accidentally deleted.

Add New Programs

The second option on the Add/Remove Programs utility is the Add New Programs option. This option assists you in installing new programs such as Microsoft Office. Installing a program using this option allows Windows 2000 to track and manage its installation.

Similar functionality is provided by the Windows 98 and Windows NT version of the Add/Remove Programs utility except that Windows 2000 Professional provides the Windows Installer Service which is a more reliable application management environment.

Installing a new application on a Windows 2000 Professional computer involves the following steps:

1. Select the **Add New Programs** option on the Add/Remove programs dialog.

2. Click on the **CD or Floppy** button. The Install Program From Floppy Disk or CD-ROM dialog appears.

3. Insert the CD-ROM or diskette that contains the program and click on **Next**.

4. Follow the instructions that appear on the screen.

Another feature provided by the Add New Programs options is the Add programs from Microsoft option. This option is useful only if the computer has access to the Internet. Clicking on the Windows Update button will instruct Windows 2000 Professional to contact the Microsoft Windows 2000 Update web site. Once the web site has been connected, the Administrator is presented with a list of software updates, fixes and utilities available for download and automatic installation.

NOTE: *Windows Update can also be started from the Start menu.*

Add/Remove Windows Components

The third option on the Add/Remove Programs utility is the Add/Remove Windows Components. This option allows you to install optional Windows components using the Windows Component Wizard that were not installed as part of the Windows 2000 Professional installation. Similar functionality is provided on the Windows Setup property sheet of the Windows 98 and Windows NT Add/Remove programs utilities.

Use the following steps to install an additional component on a Windows 2000 Professional computer:

1. Select the **Add/Remove Windows Components** option on the Add/Remove programs dialog. Windows displays a message indicating that it will take a few moments for this process to start. The Windows Components Wizard then appears.

2. Click on **Next** to continue.

3. Select one or more components from the Components list. A description of the selected component as well as its required disk space will be displayed at the bottom of the dialog. If the component to be installed consists of one or more sub-components, the Details button will become enabled. Clicking on this option with produce a dialog of sub-components and will allow you to select which sub-components should be installed. Click on **Next** to continue.

4. Windows will display a status of the component installation process. Windows 2000 will request the Windows 2000 CD-ROM. After inserting the CD-ROM click on **OK** to continue.

5. The Windows Components Wizard completes the installation process. Click on **Finish** and then on **Close**.

NOTE: *Depending on the component that you install, additional configuration may be required before it is ready for use.*

Managing User and Group Accounts

Windows 2000 utilizes user accounts to identify and manage users. Windows 2000 will not allow you to logon to the computer without authenticating your user name and password during the login process.

What you are allowed to do after that depends on the permissions that have been assigned to you. Windows 2000 allows individual user accounts to be assigned to group accounts that have their own unique set of permissions. If a large number of users share your computer, it is much easier to manage them by assigning them to a few groups and managing security permissions for the group than to try and manage every individual user.

By default the user account that is created during the installation of Windows 2000 is made a member of a group called the Power Users group. This group membership allows you to modify your computer and install applications while restricting you from accessing files that belong to other users who share the computer. There may be times when you wish to do something and do not have the necessary permissions. In this case you can either logon using the Administrator account or add your user account to the Administrators group. Membership in the Administrators group makes your account very powerful. For example, it allows you to access any file on the computer even if it does not belong to you.

NOTE: *To add an account to the Administrators group, you must use the Administrator account.*

User and group accounts are managed by the User and Passwords utility on the Windows 2000 Control Panel. From there you can add and delete user accounts, modify then, change user passwords and set group membership. By default the following groups are available:

- **Administrators**. This group has complete access to all system resources.

- **Backup Operators**. This group has the ability to backup and restore files on the computer.

- **Guests**. This group is very restricted and has the least access of any group.

- **Power Users**. This group can make modifications to the computer and install applications.

- **Replicator**. This is a special group used only by Windows 2000 for administrative purposes.

- **Users**. This group can run applications and save their work but cannot make system wide changes.

Once a user account has been made a member of a group account, the user account automatically inherits all the permissions assigned to the group. A detailed discussion of Windows 2000 security model is beyond the scope of this book, but a brief description is provided below.

There are two types of security available on Windows NT: share and NTFS. Share security controls what type of access network users are granted to local computer resources and is discussed further in Chapter 5. NTFS security is only available if you installed NTFS as your computer's file system. It governs the access granted to Windows resources for both local and network users. You can apply NTFS security by right clicking on a Windows resources, such a driver, folder or file, selecting Properties and clicking on the Security property sheet. From here you can assign or remove user and group accounts to the resource and specify the type of access that will be allowed. Available permissions include:

- Full Control

- Modify

- Read & Execute

- List Folder Contents (not available for files)

- Read

- Write

Chapter 3

Working With the Desktop

The Windows 2000 Desktop

The Windows 2000 desktop has been greatly enhanced and provides many new features. These include support for active desktop, an intelligent Start menu and a host of new toolbars.

Overview of the Windows 2000 Desktop

The Windows 2000 desktop is very similar to the Windows 98 and Windows NT desktop as shown in Figure 3.1, although the Windows 98 desktop provides a closer feature match. All three operating systems provide certain basic components, including:

47

- **Taskbar**. Appears at the bottom of your screen and contains the Start button, tool bars, the system tray and buttons for each open application.

- **Start Menu**. A menu system accessed using the Start button on the task bar which provides menu access to your files, programs and help.

- **Recycle Bin**. A utility that stores deleted files and folders until either you empty the bin or the system clears it.

- **Internet Explorer**. A program that is used for browsing your local intranet or the world wide web.

- **My Computer**. A folder that provides quick access to local drives and mapped network drives. It also contains a link to the Windows 200 Control Panel where you can configure most of your system settings.

On top of these common desktop features, Windows 2000 and Windows 98 also provide the following components:

- **My Documents**. A folder which serves as the default storage location for all your files and graphics which helps you centrally store and manage all your personal data.

- **Support for active desktop**. A desktop feature that allows you to configure your desktop to look like a web page. You can even add web content and have it automatically updated when you are logged onto the Internet.

One big difference between the Windows 2000 Professional desktop and the Windows 98 and Windows NT desktop is the My Network Places icon which replaces the Network Neighborhood. The My Network Places folder is more powerful than the Network Neighborhood and includes such additional features as the ability to store shortcuts to web and FTP sites and a link to the Network Connections Wizard.

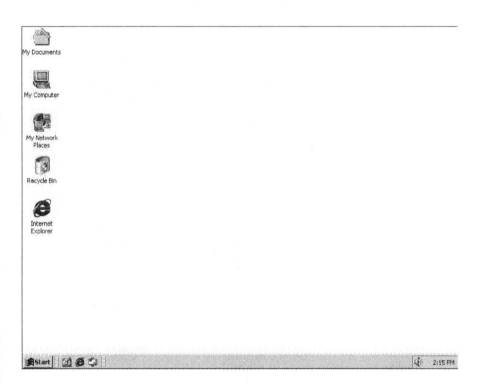

Figure 3.1 The Windows 2000 Professional Desktop

Adding Active Desktop Objects

Thanks to the integration with Internet Explorer, both Windows 98 and Windows 2000 Professional support Active Desktop. This feature allows these operating systems to display web content directly on the Windows desktop. You can even set it up so your web content is automatically updated.

In addition to Active Desktop channels you can find on the web, Microsoft provides multiple free channels via its Internet Active desktop gallery that you can set up. By default, Windows 2000 enables the Active Desktop. You can enable and disable this feature by right clicking on anywhere on the Windows desktop, selecting Active Desktop and clicking on Show Web Content.

NOTE: *You can also manage Active Desktop from the Web property sheet on the Display utility or from the General property sheet on the Folder options dialog, both of which are located in the Windows 2000 Control Panel.*

Use the following procedure to add new web content to your desktop:

1. Right-click on an open area of your desktop and select **Active Desktop** from the pop-up menu.

2. Select **New Desktop Item**. The New Desktop Item dialog appears as shown in Figure 3.2.

3. Click on the **Visit Gallery** button. You also have the option of typing the URL of a web site that provides active desktop content.

4. The Microsoft Windows Technologies Active Desktop gallery appears as shown in Figure 3.3. Browse this site to find active desktop content and then click on the **Add to Active Desktop** button. When prompted for confirmation click on **Y**es.

5. You may be prompted for additional information. When completed the active desktop content will appear directly on your Windows 2000 desktop.

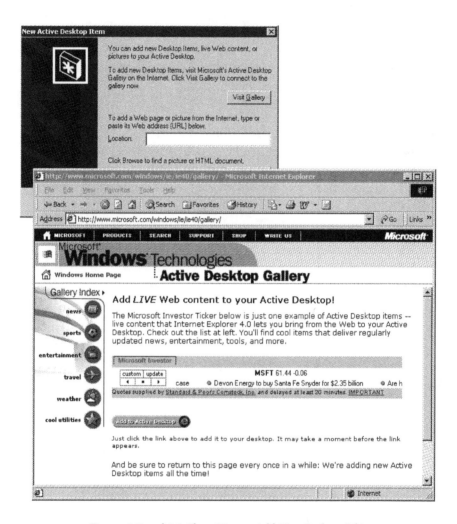

*Figures 3.2 and 3.3 Show How to Add New Desktop Objects
From Microsoft's Active Desktop Gallery*

Managing Active Desktop Objects

Managing your active desktop objects includes such tasks as:

• Enabling and disabling active objects

• Manually synchronizing active objects

• Removing active objects

To enable active objects without deleting them right-click on an open area of your desktop and select Active Desktop. At the bottom portion of the pop-up dialog that appears, you will see a list of your active objects. Objects with a check mark are currently enabled. Select an object to switch its status from one state to another.

You can manually force Windows 2000 to update all your active objects by synchronizing with the Internet. Right-click on an open area of your desktop and click on Active Desktop and then select Synchronize. A dialog appears showing the synchronization status as shown in Figure 3.4.

If you no longer need an active desktop object you can delete it. This is done by selecting the object and clicking on the Delete button on the Web property sheet of the Display properties dialog as shown in Figure 3.5. You can view additional information about active objects, control their synchronization schedule or even download the contents of their home web sites by selecting a active object and clicking on the Properties button.

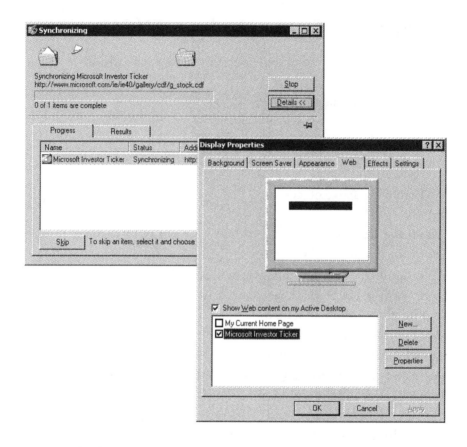

Figures 3.4 and 3.5 Demonstrate How to Synchronize and Manage Active Desktop Objects

Navigating Windows 2000 Professional

Windows 2000 Professional does something no Microsoft operating system has ever done before. It pays attention to you and the way you work and adjusts the Programs sub-menu on the Start menu so that programs which you use most often are easily found while those you use less often are hidden from view

Personalized Menus

The hidden programs on the Programs menu are still there and can be accessed by clicking on the down arrow at the bottom of the menu as demonstrated in Figure 3.6. If you decide that you do not care for personalized menus, you can disable them by selecting Start, Settings and then Taskbar & Start Menu. This opens the Taskbar and Start Menu Properties dialog. Clear the Use Personalized Menus option and click on OK. Windows 2000 will now display the Programs menu in the traditional manner.

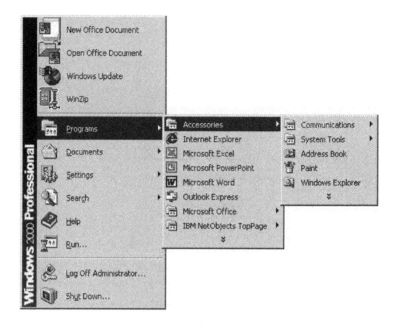

Figure 3.6 Personalized Menus Reduce Clutter and Increase Efficiency

Task Bar and Start Menu Properties

The familiar Windows NT Taskbar has been renamed Taskbar and Start Menu in Windows 98 and Windows 2000. Despite the name change, the Windows 98 version looks like and provides the same functionality as the Windows NT version. The Windows 2000 version greatly expands the capabilities of this option. It is opened by selecting Start, Settings and then Taskbar and Start Menu.

At first glance the Windows 2000 Taskbar and Start menu Properties dialog, shown in Figure 3.7, does not seem to have changed much. It still consists of two property sheets. The General sheet still provides the same basic set of controls but also adds the Use Personalized menus option, which allows you to enable and disable the use of Windows 2000 intelligent program menu.

The Advanced property sheet, shown in Figure 3.8, adds the Re-sort button to the Customize Start Menu section. This option instructs Windows 2000 to rearrange the programs on the Programs menu to their default order.

The bottom portion of the Advanced properties sheet contains an entirely new feature. This is the Start Menu Settings, and it contains the following options.

- Display Administrative Tools

- Display Favorites

- Display Logoff

- Expand Control Panel

- Expand My Documents

- Expand Network and Dial-Up Connections

- Expand Printers

- Scroll the Programs menu

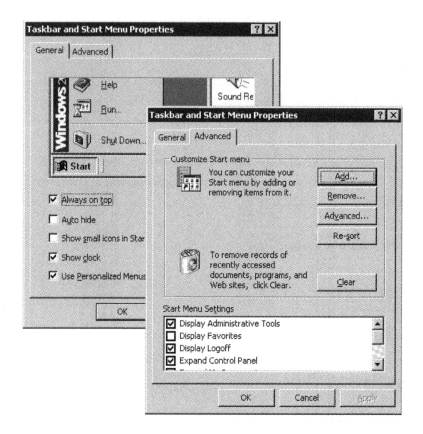

Figures 3.7 and 3.8 Show the General and Advanced Property Sheets on the Taskbar and Start Menu Properties Dialog

Quick Launch Bar

For many users the Quick Launch Bar made its first appearance on Windows 98 although it has long been available to Windows NT users as part of the Internet Explorer 4 install.

The Quick Launch Bar is the first set of icons on the Windows 2000 Taskbar. It lets you start applications with a single mouse click. The Quick Launch Bar also includes the Show Desktop icon which allows you to toggle the contents of your desktop to and from the task bar in a single click.

On Windows 2000 Professional the Quick Launch Bar is enabled by default. If you do not see it on your desktop you can turn it on by right clicking on an open area on your Taskbar and selecting Toolbars and then clicking on Quick Launch as demonstrated in Figure 3.9.

Figure 3.9 Enabling the Quick Launch Bar

By default Windows 2000 Professional places the following links on the Quick Launch Bar:

• Show Desktop

• Internet Explorer

• Outlook Express

You can add or remove links to other application by dragging and drooping them on or off of the Quick Launch Bar.

Additional Toolbars

The Quick Launch bar is actually only one of several new toolbars available on Windows 2000 Professional. Unlike the Quick Launch Bar these other toolbars are not enabled by default. These new toolbars include:

- **Address toolbar.** Allows you to quickly access a web page by typing its address.

- **Links toolbar.** Allows you to access the same links that you have stored on your Links bar in Internet Explorer.

- **Desktop toolbar.** Allows you to put all of the icons on your desktop onto this toolbar for single click access.

- **My documents toolbar.** Allows you to place the contents of your My Documents folders on a toolbar.

These tools are also available on Windows 98 except for the My document toolbar which is new with Windows 2000. These toolbars are also available to Windows NT users running Internet Explorer 4.

To enable any of these toolbars right-click on an open area on the Windows 2000 Taskbar and select Toolbars, followed by the toolbar you wish to turn on. You can move any of these toolbars to a different location on the desktop by pointing to the vertical bar on the left portion of the toolbar and dragging it to the desired location. Using the vertical bar you can also resize the toolbar.

You can also create your own custom toolbar by right clicking on an open area on the Windows 2000 Taskbar and selecting Toolbars followed by New Toolbar. This displays the New Toolbar dialog. Use this dialog to select any folder, and Windows will make a toolbar out if its contents.

My Computer

The My Computer icon on the Windows 2000 desktop provides the same basic functionality as its counterpart on Windows 98 and Windows NT. However there are some differences as shown in Figure 3.10.

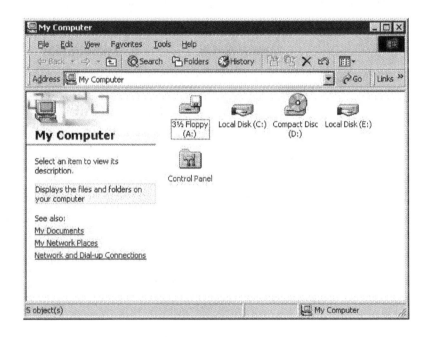

Figure 3.10 The Windows 2000 My Computer Folder

The Windows 2000 My Computer folder does not contain an icon for Dial-Up Networking like Windows 98 or Windows NT. This functionality is now provided by the Network Connection Wizard. Nor does it contain the Scheduled Task icon that Windows 98 does.

NOTE: *In Windows 2000 Scheduling is performed using the Schedule Tasks folder found at Start, Programs, Accessories, System Tools, Scheduled Tasks.*

In addition to displaying files and folders on your computer the Windows 2000 My Computer folder provides links to the following resources:

- My Documents

- My Network Places

- Network and Dial-up Connections

Like Windows 98, Windows 2000 includes the Favorites menu option which allows you to access the same favorite places stored in Internet Explorer.

The new Tools menu includes a Synchronize option for managing your offline folders. The Map Network Drive and Disconnect network Drive options have been moved here as well.

Dialog Toolbars

The integration of Windows Explorer and Windows 2000 Professional has had a positive impact on Windows 2000 and Windows 98 dialogs. These operating system dialogs now incorporate the following set of optional toolbars as demonstrated in Figure 3.11.

- **Standard Button Toolbar**. A default toolbar that facilities navigation of your computer and the Internet. Its features include back, forward and up options as well as links to Search, Folders and History options.

- **Address Toolbar.** Allows for the entry of address to computer, local area network and Internet resources.

- **Links Toolbar.** Provides access to the same links used by Internet Explorer.

- **Radio Toolbar.** Allows you to listen to Internet radio stations.

NOTE: *The Radio Toolbar is only available if you have installed the Windows Media Player and have an active Internet connection.*

To enable or disable dialog toolbars click on the View menu and select Toolbars, followed by the name of one of the available toolbars.

You can customize the Standard Button toolbar by selecting the Customize option under Toolbars on the View menu. This opens the Customize Toolbar dialog as shown in Figure 3.12. You can add or remove buttons to this toolbar by selecting them in either the Available toolbar buttons or Current toolbar buttons area and clicking on the Add or Remove buttons. You can change the position of a button on the toolbar by selecting it in the Current toolbar buttons area and clicking on either the Move Up or Move Down buttons. To reset the Standard Buttons Toolbar back to its default setting, click on the Reset button. You can also control how text should be displayed or the size of the icons using the Text options and Icon options drop-down lists.

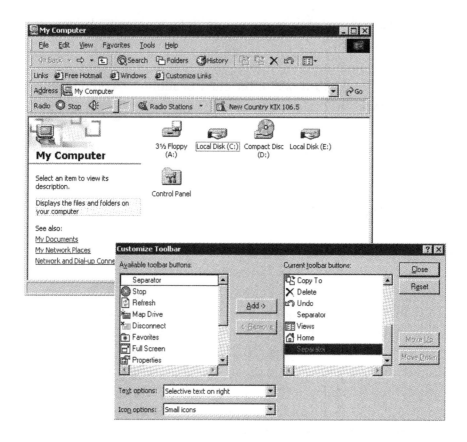

Figures 3.11 and 3.12 Demonstrate Toolbar Options and Configuration

Favorites

The ability to display Favorites from the Start menu was introduced by Windows 98. This is the same Favorites which you create and manage using Internet Explorer. This feature simply makes access to your favorite places easier. This capability has been migrated to Windows 2000, but it is not enabled by default.

To add Favorites to the Windows 2000 Start menu click on Start, Settings and then Taskbar & Start menu. Next open the Advanced tab and then select Display Favorites and click on OK. Favorites will now appear on the Start menu.

In order to manage Favorites in Windows 98 you needed to open Windows Explorer and use the Favorites menu options. In Windows 2000 you can still manage your Favorites this way, but you can also right click on Favorites from the Start menu and select Explore which will open the Favorites dialog as shown in Figure 3.13. From here you can use the Add to Favorites and Organize Favorites options in the Favorites menu to add and organize your favorites places.

The Add to Favorites option opens the Add Favorites dialog shown in Figure 3.14. From here you can create folders to manage your favorite places and add new places. You can also enable offline viewing for your favorite web site with the Make available offline option and then click on the Customize button to start the Offline Favorite Wizard where you are guided through the process of creating a synchronization schedule for the web site.

The Organize Favorites option opens the Organize Favorites dialog shown in Figure 3.15. From here you manage your favorites places. You can create new folders for managing then, rename your folders or the names of your favorites places. You can also move places from one folder to another and delete them when you do not want them anymore.

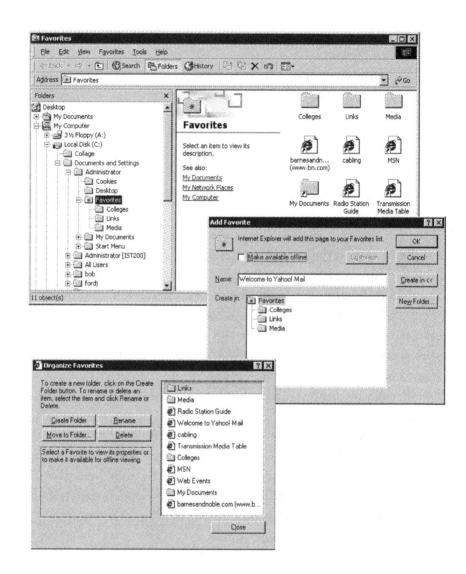

Figures 3.13—3.15 Show How to Organize and Managing Your Favorite Places

Search

Windows NT and Windows 98 both allow you to search for files and folders using the Find utility located on the Start menu. You can search by file and folder name, by modification date or for files based on size.

Windows 98 expanded the capabilities of the Find utility to include the ability to search for:

- **Files and Folders**. Look for files and folders that match your specified search criteria.
- **Computer**. Locate computers on your local area network.
- **On the Internet**. Use Internet Explorer to Find a Web page, Internet addresses, businesses or a map.
- **People**. The ability to search your personal address book or any of a list of directory services available on the Internet such as *Yahoo! People Search* for contacts or groups.

The Find utility has been greatly expanded on Windows 2000 and has been renamed Search. It be found on the Start menu and is also integrated with Windows Explorer. It provides all the functionality found in the Windows 98 Find utility. In addition, Windows 2000 includes an optional indexing service that scans your computer and builds a searchable catalog of data. To turn on the index service, open Windows Explorer and click on the Search button and then select Files or Folders under the Search for other items area as shown in Figure 3.16. Clicking on the link for the Indexing Service open the Index Service Setting dialog shown in Figure 3.17 where you can enable or disable the Index service. As this figures shows, the Windows 2000 Search dialog provides a single interface for all search options.

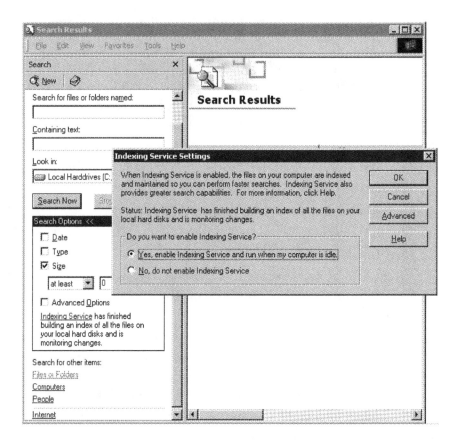

Figures 3.16 and 3.17 Show How to Enhance Searching Using the Index Service

Looking for Help

The Windows 2000 Professional help system looks very similar to the Windows 98 help system. Both provide a two-pane view. The left pane is used to present available selections, and the right pane is used to present the actual help information. This is a significant improvement over Windows NT's single pane help panel and makes help much easier to use.

Windows 2000 help is accessed by selecting Start and then <u>H</u>elp. The Help dialog is organized into the following four tabs:

- <u>C</u>ontents. Provides a listing of help topics in the form of books in the left pane. Detailed information is obtained by drilling down to specific topics which appear in the right pane.

- I<u>n</u>dex. Presents a comprehensive index of Windows help topics for you to select.

- <u>S</u>earch. Provides the ability to search Windows 2000 help based on key word searches.

- Favor<u>i</u>tes. This is an option unique to Windows 2000. It contains a list of help pages you have marked as favorites so you can easily return to them for later viewing.

Another feature only available on Windows 98 and Windows 2000 is the Web Help option which allows you to search and display web based help information. The Web Help option is located on the Help toolbar and requires an active Internet connection before it can be used. Clicking on the Web Help button displays a list of on-line help links in the left pane as shown in Figure 3.18. Clicking on any of the available options causes Windows 2000 to open Internet Explorer and connect to the web site where the help information resides.

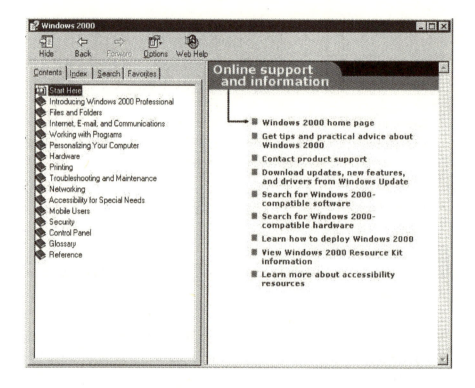

Figure 3.18 Accessing On-line Help

Windows Explorer

The Windows Explorer found in Windows NT Workstation 4.0 is considerably different from the ones found in Windows 98 and Windows 2000. Windows Explorer supports the following feature list on all three operating systems:

• Browsing and managing local and network files and folders

- Mapping and disconnecting network drivers

- Finding files and folders on local and network computers

- Managing file type association with specific applications

- Providing access to desktop objects

- Providing links to the Control Panel and Printers folder

- Integration with the Recycle bin and My Briefcase

The Windows Explorer provided by Windows 2000 and Windows 98 blurs the distinction with Internet Explorer by integrating the following list of features:

- Support for the Standard Buttons, Address Bar, Link and Radio toolbars

- Support for the Search, Favorites, History and Folders Explorer Bars

In addition, the Windows 2000 version of Windows Explorer adds the following list of features:

- The ability to synchronize and manages your offline folders

- The ability to enable active desktop

- Support for a web view of folders

- Support for single click access

- More detailed control over the display

- The ability to manage file and folder encryption

NOTE: *Windows 2000's version of Windows Explorer also includes the Thumbnail Feature which is not supported in the Windows 98 version. An explanation of the thumbnail feature is included in the next section.*

Thumbnail Views

A brand new feature introduced by Windows 2000 is the ability to browse miniature versions of graphic, web page and video files known as thumbnails stored in folders. This features is supported in several Windows dialogs including Windows Explorer, My Network Places and My Computer.

Figure 3.19 shows the thumbnail view from a folder.

The thumbnail view is one of five views available in Windows 2000 as listed below:

- Large Icons. Displays your files and folders as large icons.

- Small Icons. Displays your files and folders as small icons in row

- List. Displays your files and folders as small icons in column

- Details. Displays your files and folders as small icons in columns including information about file size, type and modification date.

- Thumbnails. Displays your graphic files as small thumbnail images while non-graphic files are displayed as large icons.

To enable thumbnail viewing open a folder that contains graphic files and then select Thumbnails from the View menu.

NOTE: *Thumbnails only work with your graphics files.*

To turn off the thumbnail view click on the View menu and select one of the other view options.

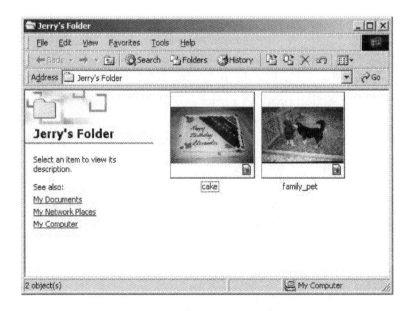

Figure 3.19 The Thumbnails View in a Folder

Windows 2000 Professional Applications

Like all Microsoft operating systems, Windows 2000 Professional comes complete with a host of useful applications and utilities. These programs can help you do everything from play games, listen to music and videos, manage your system to setting up Internet communications and video conferencing.

Accessories

Microsoft packs a lot of useful applications with Windows 2000 Professional. Many of these are common to both Windows 98 and Windows NT, and many are not. These applications are located in the Accessories folder located in the Programs menu just off the Start menu. The following section provides a brief explanation of these applications.

Accessibility. The utilities in this folder allow you to change the way Windows 2000 looks and operates for individuals who may have physical, vision or hearing problems. Available utilities include:

- **Accessibility Wizard.** Assists you in establishing optional accessibility features in Windows 2000.

- **Magnifier.** Magnifies a portion of your display making it easier to view.

- **Narrator.** Reads dialog, menu and text information on the screen.

- **On-Screen Keyboard.** Displays a graphical keyboard that you can operate with your mouse.
- **Utility Manager.** Monitors the status of other Accessibility utilities and allows you to start them and configure their automatic startup.

Communications. A collection of applications that assist you in establishing communications with other computers and networks. Available applications include:

- **Fax.** A program that turns your computer into a fax machine using its modem.

- **HyperTerminal.** A program that allows you to establish a variety of character-based connections to remote systems such as bulletin board services and Telnet sites.

- **Internet Connection Wizard.** Assists you in establishing an Internet connection with an Internet service provider.

- **NetMeeting.** This application allows you to participate in Internet meetings where you can communicate using voice, video and text.

- **Network and Dial-up Connections.** Assists you in setting up network connections with other computers, networks and the Internet.

- **Phone Dialer.** Allows you to dial and connect phone calls or to initiate Internet video conference calls via your modem and LAN connections.

Entertainment. A collection of utilities that let you listen to music CDs, watch video and record audio files.

- **CD Player**. Allows you to play compact disks using your CD-ROM drive.

- **Sound Recorder**. Allows you to record, play and edit your own audio files.

- **Volume Control**. Provides you control over the volume, treble and bass settings for your multimedia applications and systems audio.

- **Windows Media Player**. Lets you play video and audio files from local files or over the Internet.

Games. A collection of four games provided with Windows 2000 Professional.

- **FreeCell**. A card game where you try to move all the cards of the same suit into their own stack starting with the ace and ending with the king in ascending sorted order.

- **Minesweeper**. A game where the object is to uncover all the squares that do not contain hidden mines based on clues presented by neighboring squares.

- **Space Cadet 3D Pinball**. A graphical 3D pinball game which you play using your keyboard with the objective of advancing through nine levels beginning with Cadet and reaching Fleet Admiral.

- **Solitaire**. This is the same classic game of solitaire that has been available in every Windows operating system.

System Tools. A group of commonly used utilities that allow you to perform basic maintenance tasks on your computer and view configuration information.

- **Backup.** This utility lets you backup and restore your data onto other media such as disk or tape drives. This utility also allows you to create an Emergency Repair Disk you can use to fix your computer when certain problems occur which prevent it from starting.

- **Character Map.** A special collection of characters not available via the keyboard that you can insert into your documents.

- **Disk Defragmenter.** A tool for removing unused blocks of space or fragments that accumulate on your hard disks over time allowing your programs to run faster and increasing your available storage space.

- **Scheduled Tasks.** Use the Scheduled Task Wizard to help run programs and script at specified times and intervals.

- **System Information.** Organizes and provides configuration information about your computer's system, software and hardware.

Other Applications. A collection of applications included with Windows 2000 that provides a basic set of starter applications and tools for working with the operating system.

- **Address Book.** A utility that allows you to view and manage all your address contact information and which integrates with other Windows applications such as Outlook Express and NetMeeting.

- **Calculator**. A graphical utility that simulates a real calculator providing both a standard and a scientific view.

- **Command Prompt**. A window that provides a character-based interface for interacting with Windows using typed commands.

- **Imaging**. A graphics program that allows you to view and edit your graphics files.

- **Notepad**. A simple text editor for creating documents that do not require formatting.

- **Paint**. A drawing programs that allows you to create color and black and white images which can be saved as bitmap files.

- **Synchronize**. A utility that helps you schedule and manage the synchronization of your offline files.

- **Windows Explorer**. Provides access and control over files and folders on your computer and network mapped drives.

- **WordPad**. A word processor that provides basic text formatting and graphics capabilities.

Accessibility

There are five accessibility applications designed to assist users with disabilities as shown in Table 3.1.

Table 3.1 Windows Accessibility Applications

Application	Supporting Operating Systems		
	2000	98	NT
Accessibility Wizard	Yes	Yes	No
Magnifier	Yes	Yes	No
Narrator	Yes	No	No
On-Screen Keyboard	Yes	No	No
Utility Manager	Yes	No	No

NOTE: *Both Windows 98 and Windows NT provide additional support for people with disabilities with the Accessories utility located in the Windows Control Panel. Windows 2000 provides this same utility.*

The Accessibility Wizard helps you to establish optional accessibility features in Windows 2000 and does many of the things provided by the other accessibility applications. It helps you set up such things a font size, turn on the Microsoft magnifier, scroll bar and Windows border size, icon size, desktop color schemes, cursor style, turn on visual warnings to supplement audio sounds, enable speech, configure your mouse operations and shorten multiple keystroke operation to a single keystroke.

The magnifier application turns a portion of the screen into a magnified window which displays an enlarged view of a portion of the screen based on the location of the cursor, keyboard focus or area where you are editing your text. You control Magnifier Settings from the Magnifier Setting dialog shown in Figure 3.20. You can control tracking, color and presentation and set the magnification level from 1 to 9.

The Narrator application is a text to speech editor that reads your screen including menus, window contents and your own text. It works with all of the following Windows tools:

• WordPad

- Notepad

- Windows Desktop

- Internet Explorer

- Control Panel utilities

The On-Screen Keyboard application displays a graphical keyboard on your screen as shown in Figure 3.21 which you can operate via your mouse. From the Keyboard menu you can select the Enhanced or Standard keyboard, regular or block layout and or the 101, 103 and 106 keyboard types. You can enable and disable keyboard sound from the Settings menu.

The Utility Manager application, shown in Figure 3.22, lets you manage several options over your accessory applications. These options include:

- Viewing accessory application status

- Stopping and starting accessory applications

- Setting up accessory applications to automatically start when Windows or the Utility Manager starts

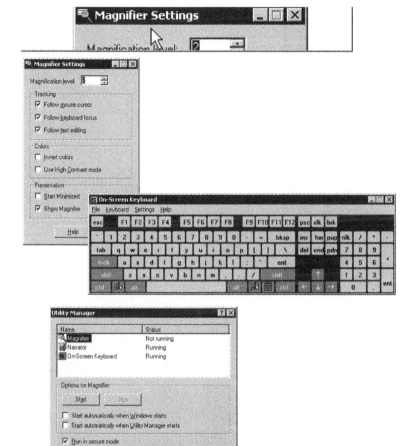

Figures 3.20—22 Demonstrate the Magnifier Application,
On-Screen Keyboard and Utility Manager

Communications

Windows 2000 Professional includes a collection of communication applications which help you to establish a variety of connections. These vary from connecting to character-based bulletin boards to the Internet and private network connections to establishing phone calls using your computer's speaker and microphone. Table 3.2 shows which of the applications are also supported in Windows NT and Windows 98.

Table 3.2 Windows Communication Applications

Application	Supporting operating systems		
	2000	98	NT
Fax	Yes	See note	No
HyperTerminal	Yes	Yes	Yes
Internet Connection Wizard	Yes	See note	No
NetMeeting	Yes	Yes	No
Network and Dial-up Connections	Yes	See note	No
Phone Dialer	Yes	Yes	Yes

NOTE: *Windows 98 does not provide the fax utility unless you already had it installed under Windows 95 when you upgraded your operating system to Windows 98.*

NOTE: *Windows 98 provides the Internet Connection Wizard as part of Internet Explorer 4.0.*

NOTE: *Windows 98's Communications folder also contains Dial-Up Networking, Dial-Up Server, Direct Cable Connection and Virtual Private networking applications which have been moved into Network and Dial-up Connections in Windows 2000.*

Fax

The Windows 2000 Professional Fax utility involves several components as shown below:

- **Fax Queue**. Allows you to view and manage outgoing faxes in a queue in the same manner that you manage your print jobs.

- **Fax Service Management**. The primary interface for working with the Fax application which allows you to enable your computer to receive faxes and to establish retry parameters, security permission and fax priorities.

- **My Faxes Folder**. The central storage location for all your sent and received faxes and fax cover pages.

- **Fax Wizard**. Steps you through the process of using the fax service.

Figures 3.23 and 3.24 show the Fax Queue and the Fax Service Management Console.

In Windows 2000 faxes can be sent from any Windows application that uses the Print command by clicking on the Fax icon in the Print dialog and clicking on the Print button. This launches the Send Fax Wizard which steps you through the rest of the process.

HyperTerminal

Both Windows 2000 and Windows 98 run the same version of HyperTerminal. Windows NT 4.0 provides an older version of HyperTerminal but it still provides the same core set of functionality. The only functional difference between the Windows 2000 and Windows 98 versions and the Windows NT version is that the newer version also support a <u>W</u>ait for a Call option on the <u>C</u>all menu. However, because HyperTerminal does not provide and automatic answer capability, you must be present to accept the call.

NetMeeting

Windows 2000 provides NetMeeting 3.01. Windows 98 provides NetMeeting 2.1. Windows NT 4.0 does not provide NetMeeting but it can be added by upgrading to Windows Explorer 4. More information on NetMeeting is available in Chapter 6.

NOTE: *Windows 98 Second edition automatically upgrades NetMeeting to version 3.0.*

Internet Connection Wizard and the Network and

Dial-up Connections

The Internet Connection Wizard and the Network and Dial-up Connections folder are new with Windows 2000. The Internet Connection on Wizard guides you through the process of establishing an Internet connection with an Internet Service provider. The Network and Dial-up Connections folder is where you go to start the Network Connection Wizard or to configure your local area network connection.

Phone Dialer

The Windows 98 and Windows NT Phone Dialer application allows you to turn your computer into a conference phone using your modem, sound card, computer speakers and microphone and to set up a series of speed dial numbers. The Windows 2000 Phone Dialer application has been substantially improved. It provides the ability to place Internet calls as well as regular phone calls and supports video conferencing if your computer has the proper hardware.

In Windows 2000 you initiate a phone call by clicking on the Dial button on the Phone Dialer toolbar and typing the phone number or IP address of the party you are calling and selecting corresponding Phone Call option and then clicking on Place Call.

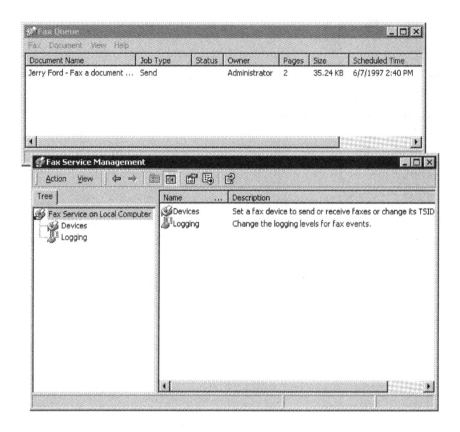

Figures 3.23 and 3.24 Show the Fax Queue and Fax Service Management Console

Entertainment

The entertainment folder contains the same set of entertainment applications found in both Windows 98 and Windows NT Workstations 4.0 as shown in Table 3.3.

Table 3.3 Windows Entertainment Applications

Application	Supporting operating systems		
	2000	98	NT
CD Player	Yes	Yes	Yes
Sound Recorder	Yes	Yes	Yes
Volume Control	Yes	Yes	Yes
Windows Media Player	Yes	Yes	Yes

While the Sound Recorder and Volume Control applications are the same for all three operating systems, the Windows 2000 Professional versions of the CD Player and the Windows Media Player have been significantly enhanced.

CD Player

The Windows 2000 CD Player has a new graphical interface as shown in Figure 3.24 which makes it look more like a real CD Player. It still performs the basic task of playing your audio CDs and allows you to store the CD title and descriptive track information. However, you no longer have to type the track information yourself. Instead Windows 2000 downloads this information from the Internet. You can set up the CD Play so that this process is automatic and you can also manually initiate it.

You configure Internet options by selecting the Preferences button and the selecting the Album Option property sheet on the CD Player Preferences dialog. To manually download track information select Internet and click on Download Track names. The Artist, title and track information is automatically displayed as soon as it is downloaded.

Windows Media Player

The Windows Media Player, shown in Figure 3.25, allows you to play audio, video and multimedia files. Unlike the Windows 98 or Windows NT Media Players, this version is fully integrated with the Internet and allows you to play live content from a web site. Options on the View menu allow you to select from three modes and two views:

Modes	Views
Standard	Full Screen
Compact	Zoom
Minimal	

Options on the Play menu allow you to control play, fast forward, rewind, skip and volume settings. The Favorites menu provides a preset list of web sites that provide media content and allows new sites to be added. The Go menu provides links to media content on the web. For example, Figure 4.26 shows the WindowsMedia.com Radio Tuner web site where you can find links to various Internet radio stations.

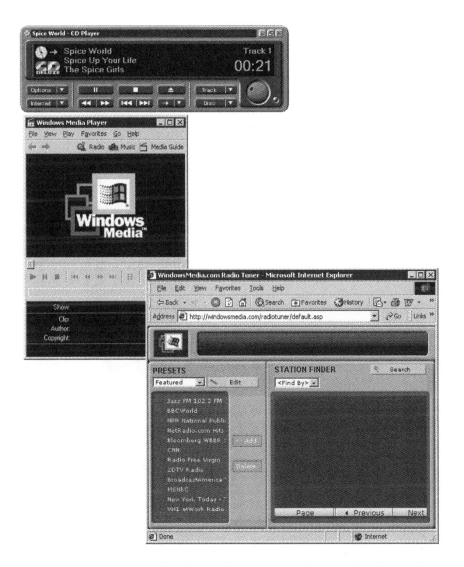

Figures 3.24—3.26 Show the Windows 2000 CD Player, Media Player and WindowsMedia.com Radio Tuner

Games

Windows operating system provide the following sets of games as shown in Table 3.4.

Table 3.4 Windows Games

Application	Supporting operating systems		
	2000	98	NT
Freecell	Yes	Yes	Yes
Minesweeper	Yes	Yes	Yes
Space Cadet 3D Pinball	Yes	No	Yes
Solitaire	Yes	Yes	Yes
Hearts	No	Yes	No

Windows NT and Windows 2000 have the same set of games. However, Windows 98 lacks Space Cadet 3D Pinball and instead provides Hearts.

If you do not see the Games folder listed on your Start menu, then the games have not been installed. To install them, open the Add/Remove Programs utility in the Windows 2000 Control Panel and click on Add/Remove Windows Components. Next double-click on Accessories and Utilities, select Games and click on OK.

System Tools

The System Tools folder provides a set of five applications which you will use to perform common maintenance tasks and view configuration information. Table 3.5 compares Windows 2000 System Tools to Windows 98 and Windows NT System Tools.

Table 3.5 Windows Systems Tools

Application	Supporting operating systems		
	2000	98	NT
Backup	Yes	Yes	Yes
Character Map	Yes	Yes	Yes
Disk Defragmenter	Yes	Yes	No
Scheduled Tasks	Yes	Yes	No
System Information	Yes	Yes	No

NOTE: *Windows NT Workstation 4.0 does not have a System Folder. It stores its equivalent programs directly in the Accessories folder.*

Backup

The Backup utility, shown in Figure 3.27, lets you backup and restore your data onto other media such as disk or tape drives in order to protect against accidental file deletion or storage media damage. Backup provides the following capabilities:

- Backup files and folders

- Restore files and folders to any available disk drive

- Schedule backups

- Create and Emergency Repair Disk or ERD

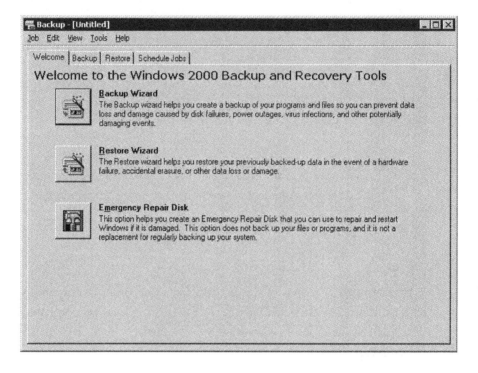

Figure 3.27 The Window 2000 Backup Utility

NOTE: *An ERD is a diskette that contains critical system files and data that you may be able to use to repair your computer when it fails to start.*

The Backup utility provides the Backup Wizard and Restore Wizard to step you through the process of managing your archived data. The Emergency Repair Disk option creates a special disk that you use to try to recover from situations in which your computer will not start.

To use the ERD insert the Windows 2000 Professional CD or the first of the four install disks and start your computer. If using floppy disks, continue to feed in disks 2,3 and 4. When prompted select the repair or recover option by typing R. Follow the instructions as presented and insert the ERD when required.

You can also manually backup and restore your files using the Backup and Restore sheets and establish a automated backup schedule on the Schedule Jobs sheet.

Character Map

Each of the three Windows operating systems has a slightly different version of the Character Map. However, all perform the same essential function and operate in a similar fashion allowing you to copy and paste special characters into your documents that are not available on your keyboard. New features in the Windows 2000 version of the Character Map include the addition of the Advanced View option, the ability to select from a wide range of character sets besides the Unicode set, and the ability to search for a special character by name, value, category and sound.

Disk Defragmenter

Microsoft has backed away from its claim that users of the Windows NT operating systems running the NTFS file system do not need to worry about disk fragmentation. Windows 2000 and Windows 98 are both equipped with such a defragmenter utility. Windows NT lacks such a tool. The Disk Defragmenter analyzes your hard disks, finding and removing unused blocks of space that accumulate over time making your system run faster and increasing available storage space. The Windows 2000 Disk Defragmenter looks different than the Windows 98 version. As shown in Figure 4.28 the top portion of the dialog displays volume information, and the Analysis display and Defragmentation display sections show detailed information. A legend at the bottom of the dialog explains the values of data. The values include:

- Red—Fragmented files

- Blue—Fragmented files

- Green—System Files

- White—Unused Space

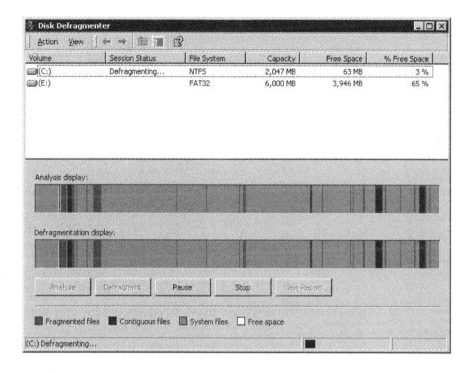

Figure 3.28 The Windows 2000 Disk Defragmenter

You click on the Analyze and Defragment buttons to examine your disk drives and optimize them. The Analyze option produces a detail report and allows you to invoke the defrag option. The Pause, Stop and Show Report buttons are enabled as the analyze and defragment processes run. The View Report option becomes available only after an analysis or defrag has been performed. You can also execute the Analyze and Defragment option from the Action menu as well as run the Pause, Stop, and View Report.

Scheduled Tasks

The Scheduled Task folder contains the Add Scheduled Task icon which you can use to start the Scheduled Task Wizard. This folder also contains icons representing any other scheduled task that you have created so that you can view and reconfigure them as required. This view is different from the Schedule Tasks dialog available on Windows 98, but otherwise the scheduling of tasks is performed in a like manner on that operating system. Windows NT does not have a scheduling option. The only way that a user can schedule a task on Windows NT is by using the At command on the Windows NT Command line.

NOTE: *Windows 2000 Professional also supports the At command.*

Using the Scheduled Task Wizard you can set up the execution of any task or application to run daily, weekly or monthly, on a one time basis, during logon and during logoff. You can specify a start time and date and schedule the days of the week that it should run. You even have the option of specifying a user name and password so that the task runs using the permission assigned to that account.

System Information

The System Information utility is common to both Windows 98 and Windows 2000. The Windows NT Diagnostics utility in Windows NT provides only a subset of the information which Windows 2000 makes available with the System Information utility.

Information is presented in categories as outlined below.

- **Resources.** Provides information about hardware (IRQs, DMA, I/O Addresses, etc.) and any resource sharing conflicts.

- **Components.** Presents information about Windows configuration settings.

- **Software Environment.** Shows all software currently running in memory.

In addition, there is a System Summary folder containing basic summary information about your computer.

NOTE: *You may see additional nodes displayed if you have applications that register themselves properly with Windows 2000.*

Two separate views are available, Basic and Advanced. You can toggle between them using their menu options on the View menu. The basic option is selected by default. The advanced option provides additional information that may be used by computer service technicians.

Other Applications

Windows 2000 Professional provides a set of applications in the Accessories folder that do not fit into any of the Applications subfolders. Several of these applications are essentially the same across Windows 98, Windows NT and Windows 2000 as shown in Table 3.6.

Table 3.6 Other Windows Applications

Application	Supporting operating systems		
	2000	98	NT
Address Book	Yes	Yes	No
Calculator	Yes	Yes	Yes
Command Prompt	Yes	Yes	Yes
Imaging	Yes	Yes	Yes
Notepad	Yes	Yes	Yes
Paint	Yes	Yes	Yes
Synchronize	Yes	No	No
Windows Explorer	Yes	Yes	Yes
Wordpad	Yes	Yes	Yes

The Calculator, Notepad, Wordpad, and Paint applications are common to all the operating systems and all operate in the same manner. Windows Explorer is also common to all three operating systems. Windows 98 introduced multiple changes with this application. Likewise, Windows 2000 has added even more new changes as explained earlier in this chapter.

The Address book application is only found in Windows 98 and Windows 2000 Professional. This application can run as a stand-alone. However, it is also integrated with several other Windows applications such as Outlook Express and NetMeeting as explained in Chapter 6.

While at first glance the Windows 2000 Command prompt in Windows 2000 and Windows NT 4.0 may resemble the Windows 98 MS-DOS prompt, there are considerable differences. Unlike Windows 98's MS-DOS prompt, this command prompt is not a true MS-DOS environment even though it supports MS-DOS like commands and you can run MS-DOS programs from it.

The Windows 2000 command prompt is the same as the Windows NT command prompt with the exception of the addition of the Find option in the Windows 2000 Edit menu which is access by right-clicking on the command prompt title bar and selecting on Edit. The MS-DOS prompt supplied with Windows 98 differs from the Windows 2000 Command prompt in several ways including:

- It lacks the Select All and Find options on the Edit menu

- It provides a graphical toolbar at the top of the Window

- It lacks the ability to configure Screen Buffer Size and Windows Size on the Layout sheet on Properties dialog

The Imaging application is included with all three operating systems. It is a graphics program that you can use to view and edit your graphics files. The only real difference between the three operating systems is that the Windows 2000 version replaces the Scan New and Select Scanner options on the File menu with the Acquire Image and Select Device options. This reflects Windows 2000's support for the latest generation of hardware including scanners and digital cameras.

NOTE: The Scanners and Cameras icon in the Windows 2000 Control assists you in installing and configuring your scanner or digital camera using the Scanner and Camera Installation Wizard.

The Windows 2000 version supports different file types than the Windows 98 or Windows NT versions as shown in Table 3.7.

Table 3.7 File Types Supported by Windows Operating Systems

File Type	Supporting operating systems		
	2000	NT	98
.tif	Yes	Yes	Yes
.awd	No	No	Yes
.bmp	Yes	Yes	Yes
.jpg	Yes	Yes	Yes
.pcx	Yes	Yes	Yes
.xif	Yes	Yes	Yes
.gif	Yes	No	Yes
.wif	Yes	No	Yes

The Synchronize option shown in Figure 3.29, starts the Synchronization Manager which assists you in scheduling and managing the synchronization of your offline files. All files and folders which you currently have set up for offline access are displayed in the main Windows pane and you can select which one you wish to synchronize. To learn more about configuring offline files refer to Chapter 4. Clicking on an offline resource and selecting Properties displays the properties dialog for that resource where you can select the Schedule property sheet and create a synchronization schedule for the offline resource. Another way to configure and manage resource synchronization is by clicking on the Setup button which opens the Synchronization Setting dialog, shown in Figure 3.30, where you can configure synchronization to occur using any of three options:

- During logon, logoff or both

- After the elapse of a period of idle time which you can specify (the default is after 15 minutes and then every 60 minutes thereafter)

- Based on a synchronization schedule which you can build using the Scheduled Synchronization Wizard

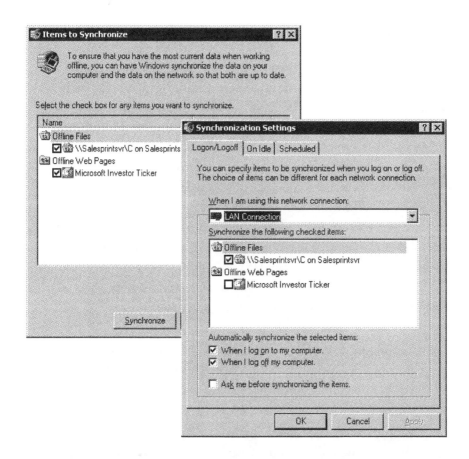

Figures 3.29 and 3.30 Demonstrate How to Manage File Synchronization

You can force an immediate synchronization by selecting which offline files you wish to synchronize and clicking on the Synchronization button.

Microsoft Management Consoles

The MMC (Microsoft Management Console) is a tool you use to help manage your computer using a standard desktop graphical interface. It was first introduced with Microsoft Internet Information Server 4 and has now been integrated into the operating system. The MMC provides a framework that provides a consistent look and feel for working with various management snap-ins. A snap-in is a component that allows you to perform a specific management task. Microsoft provides an assortment of snap-ins with Windows 2000 and has designed the operating system so that third party software developers can add new snap-ins as well. In addition to being able to create you own custom management consoles, Microsoft provides a set of predefined consoles that provide just about everything you will need to manage your own computer. These consoles are outline below:

- **Component Services**. This snap-in lets you manage COM+ applications and is typically used by software developers. It also includes snap-ins that allow you to view event logs and manage services.

- **Computer Management**. This console contains an assortment of snap-ins which allow you to manage your computer from a single desktop tool. It contains snap-ins for managing system resources, storage, services and applications, all organized in a single console tree.

- **Data Sources (ODBC)**. This service assists you in configuring your applications so that they can access whatever database you may have installed on your computer.

- **Event Viewer.** This snap-in provides administrators with access to security, application and system logs and provides equivalent functionality to Windows NT Event Viewer utility.

- **Local Security Policy.** This snap-in allows administrators to establish policies that can govern users and computers. Policies can be established to govern such things as audit, password and account lockout.

- **Performance.** This snap-in allows administrators to view an assortment of performance metrics and to analyze how the computer is managing its workload. This provides equivalent functionality to Windows NT's Performance monitor and can be used to establish benchmarks and troubleshoot performance problems.

- **Services.** Windows 2000 Professional provides basic functionality in the form of services. For example, there are services that support printing, server access and file sharing. This snap-in allows administrators to view and manage Windows services by stopping, starting and configuring them or even setting up recovery actions for service failures. It provides equivalent functionality to Windows NT's Services applet.

Chapter 4.

Working With Files and Folders

Opening and Saving Data

Microsoft has made several helpful changes to its dialog boxes which make them more intuitive and easier to work with. Improvements include such things as AutoComplete, history and icon links to common file locations.

The Open and Save Dialogs

The Windows 2000 Open and Save As Dialogs have several enhancements that make them easier to use than their Windows 98 or NT counterparts as shown in Figures 4.1 and 4.2. Something new to Windows

NT users but familiar to Windows 98 users is that these dialogs target the My Documents directory by default for storing and retrieving files.

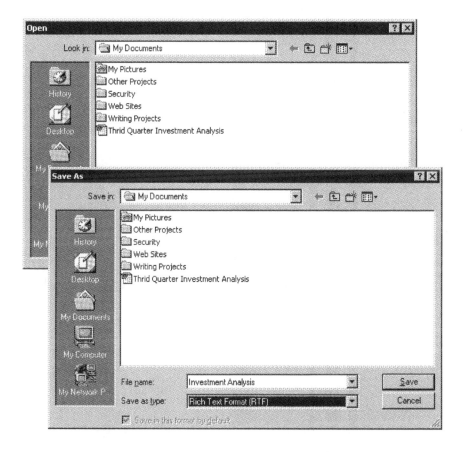

Figures 4.1 and 4.2 Show the Windows Open and Save As Dialogs

The top portion of these Windows 2000 dialogs have the familiar Look in drop down menu and buttons representing Up One Level and Create New Folder options. However, Windows 2000 has replaced the Windows 98 and NT List and Detail View buttons with a new View Menu button which provides 5 views as shown below.

- Large Icons

- Small Icons

- List

- Details

- Thumbnails

Windows 2000 also adds the Go To Last Folder Visited button which allows users to quickly return to recently visited folders.

Another new Windows 2000 feature is the five new icon shortcuts which appear on the left side of the dialog and provide fast access to local and network places where files are most commonly stored. These include:

- History

- Desktop

- My Documents

- My Computer

- My Network Places

When you select one of these shortcuts, the files and folders in that location will be displayed, and the Look in drop down list will display the selected location.

The Open With Dialog

Windows 98 and Windows NT automatically maintain a default application association for many types of files. For example, a file type of .txt is associated with the notepad application, and a file type .doc might be associated with Microsoft word. Double-clicking on a file in Windows Explorer automatically launches a associated application. In order to use a different application to work with on a file, a Windows 98 or NT user either has to first start the application and use it to open the file or select the file, press and hold the shift key and then right click on the file and select Open With.

Windows 2000 makes finding the right application to work with on a given file much easier by improving the Open With menu and allowing users to search for and use different applications than those which Windows 2000 already associates with the document type. In addition, Windows 2000 can maintain multiple application associations for each file type.

Users can right click on any file within Windows Explorer and select the Open With option from the menu that appears. They can then either select a application from the list provided or select the Choose program command and browse the computer with the Open With dialog for a application that is not listed. The next time the user returns to this or any similar type of document the application will appear in the list.

TIP!   *To set a new application as the default application for a given file type select the Always Use This Program To Open File option. Windows 2000 will automatically start application in the future when a file of the same type is opened from Windows Explorer.*

Working With Files and Folders

Microsoft has added a host of new features for managing your files. These include specialized folders for storing your document and graphics, file and folder encryption and support for offline viewing and file synchronization.

My Documents

Windows 2000 creates a My Documents folder for every Windows 2000 user and sets it as the default folder for all their documents. This helps users to centrally organize and manage all their files and folders. When users log onto a Windows 2000 machine, they only see their own My Documents folder.

While Windows 98 users are accustomed to working with the My Documents folder, this feature will be new to Windows NT users. Like Windows 98, Windows 2000 automatically places a link to each user's My Documents folder on their desktop and on the Documents submenu of the Windows Start menu. Another shortcut to this folder is located at the top of Windows Explorer.

One difference between Windows 98 and Windows 2000 is the location of the Documents folder which in Windows 2000 is usually located in C:\Documents and Settings*usersname*\My Documents. There will be a different My Documents folder for each user of the computer.

Another difference between Windows 98 and Windows 2000 My Documents folder it that the Windows 2000 folder also contains the My Pictures folder which is the default location used to store all images.

Windows 2000 Professional creates and maintains a unique My Documents folder for every user. Unlike Windows 98 which lacks NTFS security, Windows 2000 security prevents other users from being able to access each other's My Documents folder.

TIP! *To further secure the contents of your My Documents folder, consider encrypting it and all its subfolders. Also encrypt the Temp folder because Windows 2000 often uses this folder to hold copies of files while they are being edited.*

NOTE: *Some older applications may not use the My Documents folder. Pay careful attention so you do not loose track of where your work is stored when working with these applications.*

My Pictures

The My Pictures folder is a feature new to Windows operating systems. It provides a central location for users to store all of their graphic images. It resides within the My Documents Folder. The My Pictures folders allows users to view a selected image using Windows Explorer without opening it with a graphics viewer or editor as shown in Figure 4.3.

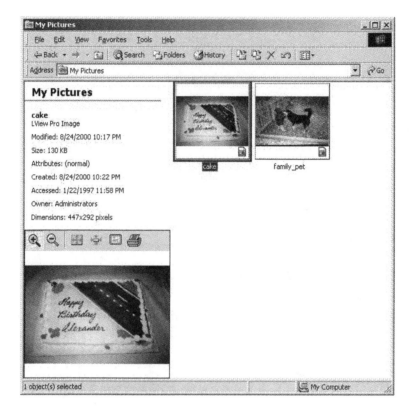

Figure 4.3 Previewing a Image Using the My Pictures Folder

In addition, the My Pictures folder provides the following features:

- Zoom In and Out

- View Actual Size

- View Best Fit size

- Full Screen Preview

- Print

Other information provided by the My Documents folder includes:

- Image Type

- Modification Date

- Image Size

- Image Attributes

- Date and Time Created

- Date and Time the Image was Last Accessed

- Image Owner

- Image Dimensions

NOTE: *Any folder can be configured to manage graphic files just like the My Pictures folder by selecting Customize this folder from the Folders' View menu. This starts the Customize This Folder Wizard which allows the users to set up the folder for image preview.*

Customizing Folders

Folder customization is a feature first introduced by Windows 98 which allows users to add a backgrounds to their folders and to control its presentation by editing an HTML template. Windows 2000 builds upon this option by adding optional folder presentation templates and allowing you to add comments about your folders which can be viewed in Windows Explorer.

To customize a folder, open it and right click anywhere in the body of the folder and select Customize This Folder from the pop-up menu that appears. The Customize This Folder Wizard appears. This wizard steps the user through the folder customization process. Three customization options are available as shown in Figure 4.4.

If the Choose or edit an HTML template for this folder option was selected, Windows 2000 will present a list of 4 presentation templates from which the user may choose or edit as shown in Figure 4.5. If you choose the Modify background picture and filename appearance option, a dialog similar to Figure 4.6 appears allowing you to use any .bmp, .gif, .jpg, .dib, .htm as the folder's background. The Add Folder comment option allows you to add a comment about the content of the folder as demonstrated in Figure 4.7.

TIP! *The Folder options utility in the Windows 2000 Control Panel provides another means of customizing folders. Changes made here affect all folders including the My Documents folder. From here you can control such features as whether Windows 2000 uses a single window or cascades windows as you work or whether a folder opens with a single or double click. You can also specify how files are presented and enable offline files.*

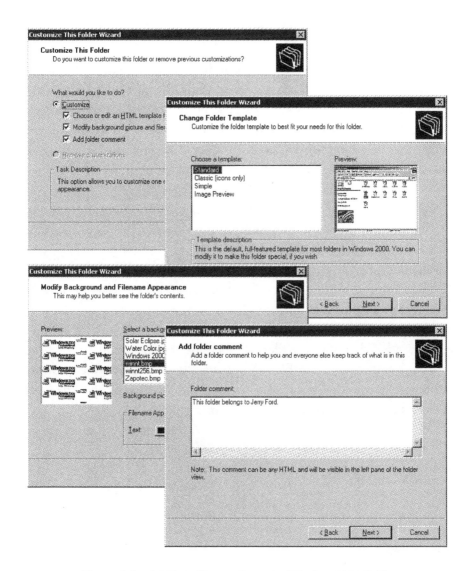

Figures 4.4—4.7 Show How to Customize Windows 2000 Folders

File and Folder Encryption

File and folder encryption is a new Windows operating feature. Encrypting a file makes it more secure. Only the user who encrypted it will be able to access it. Other users may be able to browse the user's encrypted files and folders but will not be able to open them. File and folder encryption is transparent to the user and once it has been established the user will not notice any difference when working with them.

NOTE: *Encryption is only available if the disk volume has been formatted with NTFS 5.*

You encrypt a file by right clicking on it, selecting Properties, clicking on the Advanced button on the General tab and then selecting Encrypt contents to secure data as shown in Figure 4.8. After clicking on OK twice Windows 2000 displays the dialog shown in Figure 4.9 warning that it is recommended that both the files and its folder be encrypted.

When you encrypt a file, Windows 2000 displays the Confirm Attribute Changes dialog asking whether it should encrypt only the folder or all files and subfolders in it as shown in Figure 4.10.

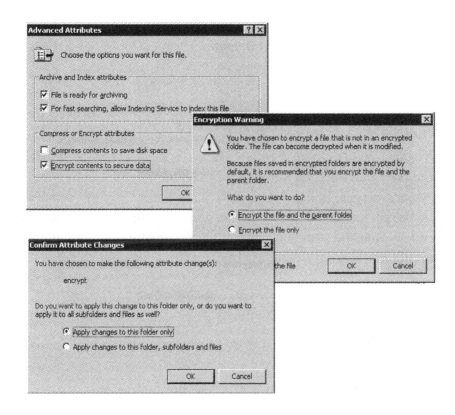

Figures 4.8—4.10 Demonstrate How to Establish File Encryption

TIP!   *You can test encryption by logging off and back on with a different user account and trying to access the encrypted file or folder.*

TIP!   *To protect your data, encrypt the My Document folders and the Temp directory. Sometimes Windows 2000 places copies of documents in the Temp directory while they are being edited.*

TIP!   *Be careful when moving around encrypted files and folder. If you copy a encrypted file to a non-NTFS 5 disk volume, the file will not be encrypted in its new location, and if you send a copy of a file out over a network, it will not be encrypted.*

Offline Files and Folders

Windows 2000's Offline Files and Folders is an alternative to Windows 98 and NT's Briefcase. You can establish an offline file or folder by selecting the Make Available Offline option on a file or folder's pop-up menu. The first time that you make a file or folder available offline, the Offline Files Wizard executes and steps you through the process of establishing your first offline file or folder. Among the available configuration options are:

- Automatically synchronize offline files at logon and logoff

- Alert when the network copy of a offline file or folder is unavailable

- Create a shortcut for the offline folder on the desktop

Windows 2000 displays offline files and folders with a small double arrow marker at the bottom left corner of file or folder's icon as shown in Figure 4.11.

The next time your create an offline file, Windows 2000 marks it as an offline file. When you create your next offline folder, Windows 2000 presents the Confirm Offline Subfolders dialog as shown in Figure 4.12. This dialog allows you to choose whether just the folder itself should be made available offline or whether all its subfolders should also be made available offline as well.

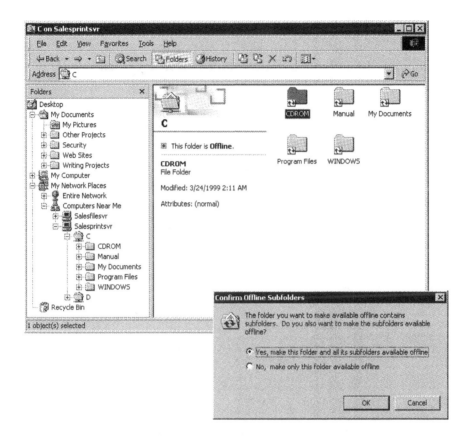

Figures 4.11 and 4.12 Show How to View and Manage Offline Folders

Windows 2000 always attempts to access the network files and folders first. If you try to access a file or folder that has been marked as offline and the network connection to it is not available, Windows 2000 will access the local copy of the offline resource and make it appear that it is in the same location as its real network counterpart.

Whenever you try to work with a offline file or folder which is not available on the network, Windows 2000 displays a icon representing the owning network computer in the task bar and displays a notification screen tip. You can double-click on this icon to display the Offline Files Status dialog, which shows the status of the connection and allows you to try and synchronize local files with offline resources when the network copy is once again available.

By default Windows 2000 automatically attempts to synchronize your offline files and folders every time you log on and off. You can also manually synchronize by selecting Synchronize from the Tools menu in Windows Explorer to open the Items to Synchronize dialog. Clicking on the Synchronize button instructs Windows 2000 to compare each offline resource to its corresponding network resource. The Setup button on this dialog opens the Synchronization Settings dialog where you can establish other configuration options.

Some additional things to remember about offline files and folders include:

- If a file is deleted or added to an offline folder, it will be deleted or added to the corresponding network folder during synchronization

- If both local and network copies of a offline file have been changed, Windows 2000 will prompt you to pick the more current one or allow you to keep both by renaming the local copy.

TIP!   *Windows 2000 automatically enables the use of offline files and folders. You can disable or configure this feature by selecting the Offline Files tab in the Folder Options utility found on the Control Panel.*

NOTE: *Windows 2000 still provides the Briefcase feature which can be access by opening a folder, right clicking and selecting Briefcase.*

Chapter 5

Networking

Setting Up Network Connectivity

Windows 2000 is the best network client that Microsoft has ever produced. With features like plug and play network interface card installation and automatic IP addressing, it participates as easily on peer networks as it does on large client/server networks.

Naming Your Computer, Workgroup and Domain

In Windows 98 the computer name and network workgroup are configured on the Identification property sheet of the Network Dialog which is opened from the Windows 98 Control Panel. To configure domain access you use the Configuration property sheet on the Network dialog to locate and select the Client for Microsoft Networks and then click on the Properties button.

In Windows NT you can view the computer's name, workgroup membership and domain access on the Identification property sheet on the Network dialog which you opened from the Windows NT Control Panel. To configure any of these settings you must click on the Change button to open the Identification Changes dialog.

Windows 2000 Professional does not provide a Network dialog in its Control Panel. To configure your computer's name, workgroup and domain information, you need to open the System icon on the Windows 2000 Control Panel and access the Network Identification property sheet as shown in Figure 5.1.

You can directly edit any of the three settings by clicking on the Changes button which opens the Identification Changes dialog as shown in Figure 5.2. You can also click on the Network ID button to start the Welcome to the Network Identification Wizard. This wizard steps you through the process of connecting to a peer network or domain.

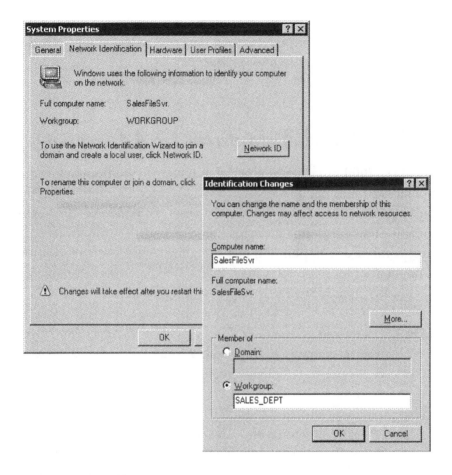

Figures 5.1 and 5.2 Show How to Change Computer Name and Network Membership

NOTE: *To join a domain your network administrator will have to create a domain user account for both you and your computer in order for you to get connected. Make sure you have this information before trying to join the domain.*

NOTE: *Any changes you make to your computer name, workgroup or domain membership will require a restart of your computer before they become effective.*

TCP/IP and Automatic IP Addressing

Windows 2000 Professional provides automatic IP addressing for small computer networks that do not have a DHCP server. This feature was first introduced with Windows 98 and is new to Windows NT users. Automatic IP addressing is great for home and small business networks because combined with plug and play it automates the configuration and establishment of local area networks. It also automates the setup of computers on corporate networks that deploy DHCP servers.

NOTE: *A DHCP server is a Windows NT or Windows 2000 Server running the DCHP service. This service listens for computers requesting IP configuration information so that they can connect to the network and leases IP addresses and other configuration information to these network clients from a pool of IP addresses which have been set up by the network administrator. The benefit of DHCP on large networks it that it alleviates the network administrator of the responsibility of having to visit and configure static IP address and configuration information for every network computer.*

When Windows 2000 discovers a plug and play network card, it automatically installs and configures local area network access for the computer. One of the default settings is to look for a DHCP server for an IP address assignment as shown in Figure 5.3. On a small network without a DHCP server, Windows 2000 will automatically assign its own IP configuration after it fails to find a DHCP server. If your network has a DHCP server, Windows 2000 will contact it and request IP configuration information which it will then use to establish its network connection. Either way your local area network connection should be automatic.

When Windows 2000 Professional configures its own IP settings, it automatically assigns itself an IP address for a class B network of 169.254.0.0 network in the range of 169.254.0.1 to 169.254.255.254 with a subnet mask of 255.255.0.0. Figure 5.4 shows the results of a *IPCONFIG /ALL* command which instructs Windows to display its TCP/IP configuration settings. In this case the computer has been configured for automatic configuration of IP information and has assigned itself an IP address of 169.254.50.179.

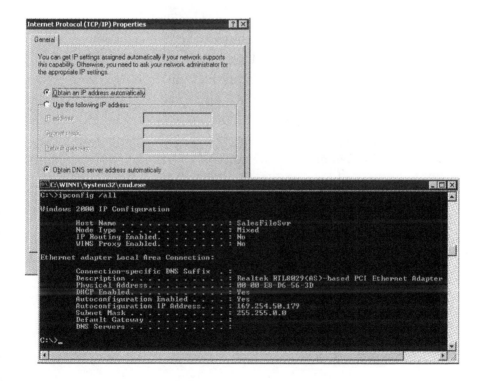

Figures 5.3 and 5.4 Show How to Configure and View TCP/IP Settings

NOTE: *If your network uses static IP addresses, you will need to turn automatic IP addressing off and configure TCP/IP with an IP configuration provided by your network administrator provides. To configure your local area network connection, select Start, Settings, Network and Dial-up Connections, Local Area Connection and then select the Properties button.*

Introducing the Network Connection Wizard

The Network Connection Wizard provides a vastly improved means for creating network connections compared to Windows 98 or NT. In Windows 98 virtual private networking and client and server dial-up connections are created and managed from the Dial-Up Networking Folder. PC to PC direct connections are handled from the Direction Cable Connection Wizard. In Windows NT, the Dial-Up Networking utility in the My Computer dialog supports client and server dial-up communications. PC to PC connections are established via the modems utility. Establishing a virtual private network connection requires multiple steps including the installation of the Point to Point Protocol on the network dialog, the configuration of the RAS service to include a VPN device and the creation of two phone book entries. Windows 2000 Professional consolidates the creation of all these different types of network connections into the Network Connection Wizard.

The Network Connection Wizard

The network Connection Wizard is started by double-clicking on the Make New Connection icon on the Network and dial-up connections folder. It provides a central location for defining and managing all network locations including:

- **Dial-up to private network.** Steps you through the process of connecting to a private network using a modem or ISDN line.

- **Dial-up to the Internet.**Assists you in creating a dial-up connection with your Internet Service Provider.

- **Connect to a private network through the Internet.** Allows you to connect to a private network by first dialing into your Internet Service Provider and then connecting to the remote network using encrypted communications.

- **Accept incoming connections.** Allows you to turn your computer into a dial-up server supporting phone, Internet and direct PC to PC connections and to allow access to local computer resources or to setup your computer as a gateway to a local network.

- **Connect directly to another computer.** Allows the establishment of temporary connections between two computers via a serial, parallel or infrared connections.

Dial-Up To Private Network

Both Windows 98 and NT support dial-up client network connections. In Windows 98 you create a dial-up connection from the Dial-Up Networking folder by double-clicking the Make New Connection icon which starts the Make New Connection Wizard. In Windows NT you must first install the TCP/IP protocol and the Remote Access Service and then create a new phone entry in the RAS phone book by double-clicking on the Dial-Up Networking icon in My Computer. In Windows 2000 Professional dial-up connections to private networks are created via the Network Connection Wizard.

The process of creating a dial-up connection to a private network in Windows 2000 is almost identical to that of Windows 98. The one exception is Windows 2000 includes the ability to create the dial-up connection and share it with all users of the computer.

You will need to know three things before creating your dial-up connection:

- The phone number of the remote dial-up server

- Your user and password on the remote network

- The protocols supported on the remote network

Use the following procedure to set up a dial-up connection:

1. Start the Network Connection Wizard by double-clicking on the Make New Connection icon in the Network and Dial-up Connection folders.

2. Click on **Next** when the welcome screen appears.

3. Select the **Dial-up to Private Network** option and click on **Next**.

4. The Phone Number to Dial screen appears. Type the phone number for the network and click on **Next**.

5. Select either the **For all users** or **Only for myself** option and click on **Next**.

6. Finally type a name for your new dial-up connection and click on **Finish**.

Windows 2000 places an icon for your new connection in the Network and Dial-up Connection folder.

Once created you can configure your dial-up connection by right-clicking on it and selecting Properties. The properties dialog for your connection appears. By default Windows 2000 Professional creates a Point to Point protocol connection and binds the TCP/IP protocol and the Client for Microsoft Networks. This is all you will probably need to dial into any Microsoft based network that supports remote access.

NOTE: *The Point to Point protocol or PPP is a protocol designed to support wide area network communications with private networks or the Internet.*

If the network for which you are creating the dial-up connection does not support TCP/IP, you will need to install the appropriate protocol which is done by clicking on the Install button on the Dial-up Connection's Property dialog.

Dial-Up To The Internet

In Windows 2000 Professional a dial-up connection to the Internet is created by choosing the Dial-up to the Internet option in the Network Configuration Wizard in Windows 2000. This starts the Internet Connection Wizard. This wizard is very similar to the Internet Connection Wizard in Windows 98. To connect to the Internet in

Windows NT you must install the TCP/IP protocol and the RAS service and then configure a phone book entry for your ISP.

The Internet Connection Wizard provides three options:

- **I want to <u>s</u>ign up for a new Internet account.** Assists you in locating and signing up with an Internet Service Provider or ISP and configuring your Internet access.

- **I want to transfer my <u>e</u>xisting Internet account to this computer.** Assists you in setting up Internet access when you already have an account with an ISP.

- **I want to set up my Internet connection <u>m</u>anually, or I want to connect through a local area network (LAN).** Allows you to manually configure an Internet connection to your ISP in much the same manner as you do when creating a dial-up connection to an private network. It also helps you to establish an Internet connection by locating and connecting to a network proxy server.

NOTE: *A proxy server is a computer or other network device that shares its connection to the Internet or other private network. It transmits and receives information to the Internet on behalf of other local network computers using its own Internet IP address.*

Connect To A Private Network Through the Internet

A virtual private network is a special type of dial-up connection that allows you to connection to a private network using the Internet in place of dialing directly into the private network.

In Windows 98 a virtual private network is configured from the Dial-Up Networking folder. In Windows NT, establishing a virtual private network connection requires multiple steps including the installation of the Point to Point Protocol on the network dialog, the configuration of the RAS service to include a VPN device and the creation of two phone book entries. Windows 2000 Professional simplifies the creation of a VPN connection with the Connect to a Private network through the Internet option in the Network Configuration Wizard.

Windows 2000 Professional supports two protocols for VPN connections, the Point to Point Tunneling Protocol and the Layer Two Tunneling Protocol. Your VPN connection is encrypted so that your data is only readable by the authenticating VPN server. Like other connections, VPN connections are located in the Network and Dial-up Connections folder. To create a VPN connection:

1. Double-click on the Make New Connection icon in the Network and Dial-up Connections folder and click on **N**ext.

2. Select Connect to a private network through the Internet and click on **N**ext.

3. Select **Automatically dial this initial connection** and the select a existing dial-up connection to your ISP and click on **N**ext.

4. Enter either the IP address or the host name of the VPN server to which you want to connect and click on **N**ext.

5. Select either **F**or all users or **O**nly for myself depending on whether or not you want to allow other users to use the VNP connection and click on **N**ext.

6. Enter a name of the connection and click on **Finish**.

Once you have defined your VPN connection, you can connect to it by double-clicking on its icon. If you are not currently connected to the Internet you will be prompted to connect using an existing dial-up connection. You will then be prompted to provide a user name and password that is valid on the VPN server to which you are trying to connect.

Accept Incoming Connections

The Accept Incoming Connections option on the Network Connection Wizard allows you to turn your Windows 2000 Professional computer into a remote access server, allowing other computers to connect to your computer via one of the following methods:

- Phone line

- Internet (VPN)

- Direct Cable Connection

Windows 2000 Professional can accept up to one of each type of connection at a time. It does not, however, support multiple instances of the same type of connection.

Both Windows 98 and Windows NT are capable of providing this same set of incoming connections. However, Windows 2000 Professional has made the process of establishing them more intuitive.

The following steps are involved in configuring your incoming connection:

- Select Accept Incoming Connections when prompted by the wizard

- Pick the appropriate type of connection from the list of available options

- Determine if a VPN connection will be accepted

- Select user and group account that will be allowed to access the incoming connection

- Install and configure any networking components required to support the connection

- Provide a name for the connection

The connection that you create will be stored in the Network and Dial-up Connections folder and can be further configured by right-clicking on the connection and selecting Properties from connection's pop-up menu. The Connection's Properties dialog appears as shown in Figure 5.5. On the General property sheet you can configure any available communication device to support an incoming connection and determine if a VPN session will be supported. The Users property sheet, shown in Figure 5.6, allows you to determine which user accounts have access to the incoming connection and to specify whether or not users must encrypt their passwords and data.

NOTE: *Users who will be connecting to your computer can enable encryption on their end of the connection by selecting the Require data encryption option on the Security tab of their connection.*

The Networking property sheet allows you to add and remove and configure protocols, clients and services that are required to support the connection as shown in Figure 5.7.

Figures 5.5—5.7 Show How to Configure an Incoming Connection

Connect Directly To Another Computer

Direct PC to PC connections are supported by Windows 98, NT and 2000. While substantially slower than a conventional local area network connection, direct PC to PC connections are great for temporary connections and provide the same functionality between two computers as a regular network connection.

Windows 98 calls direct PC to PC connections Direct Cable Connections. Before you can setup one of these connections on Windows 98, Direct Cable Connections must first be installed using the Add/Remove Programs utility. Windows 98 supports connections using serial, parallel and infrared connections.

Windows NT only offers support for serial direct PC to PC connections. It must first be installed by using the Modems dialog and selecting Dial-Up Networking Serial Cable Between 2 PCs.

Windows 2000 Pro supports serial, parallel and infra red connections which are established via the Connect directly to Another Computer option in the Network Connection Wizard. Setup involves three steps as shown in Figure 5.8, 5.9 and 5.10. These are the setup of a the host or client connection, specification of the connection type and the assignment of users who will be allowed to use the connection. Once both the host and client machines have been setup, a connection can be initiated from the client side by double-clicking on the connection in the Network and Dial-Up Connection dialog.

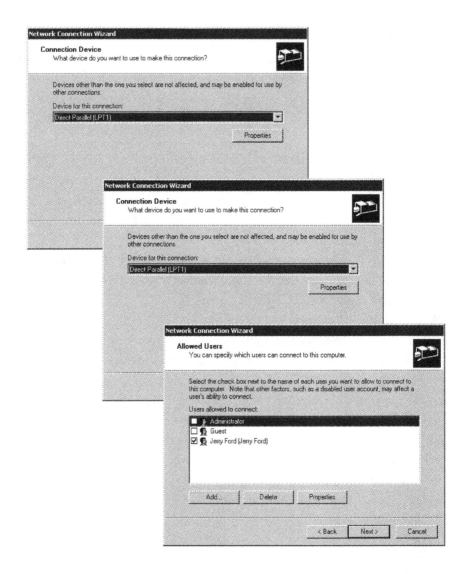

Figures 5.8—5.10 Demonstrate How to Set Up a Direct PC-to-PC Connection

By default a direct PC to PC connection gives the client access to resources on the host computer based on the user account permissions as assigned on the host system. However, the host side of the connection can be configured to also act as a gateway to a local area network that provides the client computer with full network access based upon the user network account permissions. This is done by configuring TCP/IP to accept incoming connections by selecting TCP/IP in the Network dialog and clicking on Properties and then selecting Allow callers to access my local area network as shown in Figure 5.11.

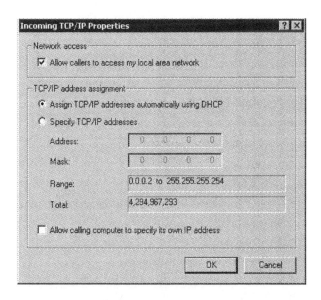

Figure 5.11 Allow Connected User to Access Your Local Area Network

Finding and Connecting to Network Resources

Windows 2000 Professional makes finding and accessing network resources easy with new features like My Network Places and the Network

Place Wizard. Windows 2000 encourages searching over network browsing and has greatly enhanced your search capabilities. However, if you prefer you may still browse the network in search of resources.

My Network Places

The My Network Places folder on the Windows 2000 Professional desktop replaces the Network Neighborhood folder used on Windows 98 and Windows NT and makes locating network resources faster.

The My Network Places folder provides a link to the Network and Dial-up Connections folder where you can configure your local area connection and launch the Network Connection Wizard. It provides two views of your network, the Entire Network and Computers Near Me. The Entire Network icon provides a view to all the computers and printers on the network. The Computer Near Me icon shows all computers which are members of your workgroup.

The Add Network Place icon launches the Add Network Place Wizard which steps you through the process of creating links to network resources which Microsoft calls Network Places as shown in Figure 5.12.

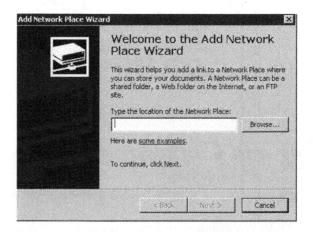

Figure 5.12 Creating a Network Place

The three types of network places are identified in Table 6.1.

Table 6.1 Methods for Linking to Network Resources

Network Place	Example text entry
Shared network folder	\\servername\sharename
Web folder on the Internet	http://webservername/sharename
FTP site	ftp://ftp.ftpservername.com

TIP! *You can also create Network Places by locating a network computer, right-clicking on it and selecting Create Shortcut from the pop-up menu.*

Network and Dial-up Connections

Network and Dial-up Connections is a new Windows feature. It is opened from either the My Network Places dialog, the Network And Dial-Up Connections icon in the Windows Control Panel or by selecting Start, then Settings and Network and Dial-up Connections.

This folder contains icons representing all network connections for the computer. Windows 2000 Professional automatically configures a local area connection when it detects an installed NIC. A network connection can be any one of the following:

- Dial-up connection to a private network

- Internet dial-up connection

- A Virtual private Network Connection

- A Incoming connection

- Direct Connection to another Computer

You can create new connections using the Make New Connection icon. You can also configure current connections by right clicking on them and selecting Properties. You can monitor your connections by right clicking on them and selecting Status, and you can enable and disable them by right clicking on them and selecting Enable or Disable. You can also get basic status information by just selecting a connection.

This dialog also provides links to the System Properties dialog where you can configure the computer name, workgroup or domain access and to the Windows Optional Network Components Wizard where you can add or remove various network applications.

Local Area Connection

Windows 2000 Professional automatically configures a local area connection for every network interface card or NIC that it finds in a computer. Therefore you will not find local area connection as an option in the Network Connection Wizard. This connection provides everything you will need to connect to and operate on a Windows local area network.

You can configure your local area connection by double-clicking on the local area connection in the Network and Dial-up connections folder. This opens the Local Area Connection Properties dialog as shown in Figure 5.13. Local area network connection configuration is much easier in Windows 2000 compared to Windows NT because Microsoft has patterned this interface after the Windows 98 network dialog. You now install and work with the same clients and services as are used in Windows 98 instead of the Windows NT services.

Microsoft has moved computer, workgroup and domain setup and configuration to the System utility thus streamlining local area network configuration. At the button of this dialog Microsoft has added the Show icon in taskbar when connected option to allow you to decide whether you want Windows 2000 to provide a visual display of your local area network connection status.

By default Windows 2000 Professional installs the following clients, services and protocols:

- **The Client For Microsoft Networks.** Allows Windows 2000 Professional to access network resources. Windows 98 also uses this client. Windows NT Workstation provides the Workstation service with similar functionality.

- **File and Printer Sharing for Microsoft Networks.** Allows Windows 2000 Professional to share local folders or even the contents of entire disk drives with other network users. It also allows Windows 2000 to share a local printer and act as a network print server.

- **Internet Protocol (TCP/IP).** TCP/IP is Microsoft's default protocol for networking. When combined with Windows 2000's new automatic IP addressing feature, it allows Windows 2000 Professional to automate network configuration.

You can configure any of the default networking options by selecting them and clicking on the Properties button. For example, Figure 5.14 shows the TCP/IP Properties dialog from which you can configure dynamic or static IP settings. You can also add or remove new clients, services or protocols by selecting the Install and Uninstall buttons.

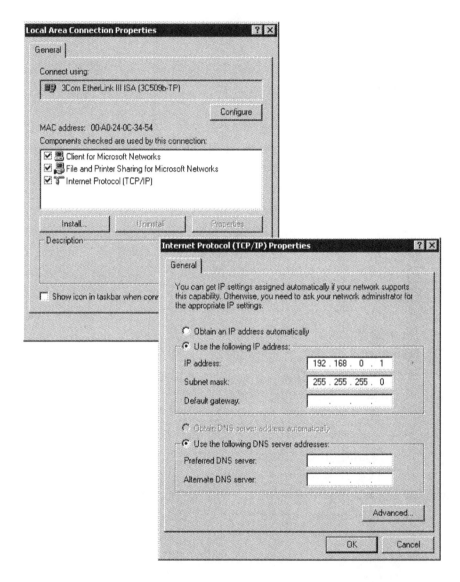

Figures 5.13—5.14 Show How to View and Configure TCP/IP Settings

NOTE: *By default Windows 2000 Professional automatically enables DHCP support for TCP/IP allowing complete automation of Windows 2000 network configuration on small peer networks and large networks that support DHCP.*

Printing

Printing in Windows 2000 Professional is very similar to printing in Windows NT and Windows 98. All these operating systems support local and network printing, manage printers from the Printer dialog and use the Add printer Wizard to install both local and network printers.

Windows 2000 borrows plug and play from Windows 98 to automate the installation of local printers. Windows 2000 and NT provide advanced print features such as printer pools and printer priorities that Windows 98 does not support.

TIP!   *If Windows 2000 Professional does not automatically detect your printer when you install it try restarting the computer.*

A printer pool can be established by attaching two print devices that use the same software driver and configuring them as one logical printer. One print queue manages all print jobs. Windows 2000 will then submit print jobs to the first available printer in the pool. Print pools are established in the Ports property sheet of the Printer's Properties dialog as shown in Figure 5.15.

Print priorities allow you to install multiple logical instances of the same physical print and assign each instance a different priority and assign network users and groups to specific instances. Windows 2000 gives preference to users who are allowed to submit print jobs to the instance with the higher priority. Print priorities are established on the Advanced property sheet of the Printer's Properties dialog as shown in Figure 5.16.

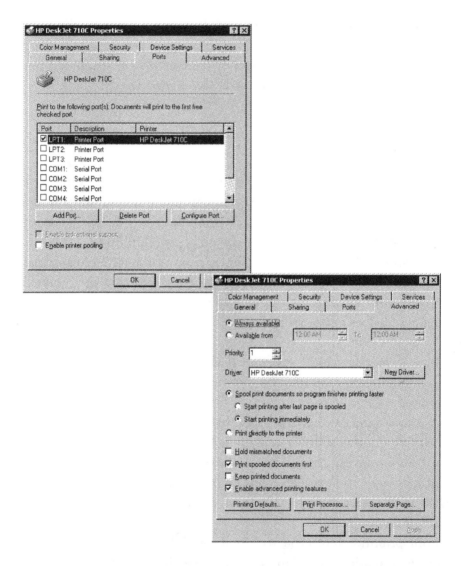

Figures 5.15 and 5.16 Show How to Establish Print Priority

Another feature that Windows 2000 and Windows NT have in common is their ability to store print drivers when creating a printer share for other operating systems. This feature is configured on the Sharing property sheet of the printer's properties dialog. When a network computer installs an instance of the shared printer, Windows 2000 will automatically download the appropriate software driver to the connecting computer based on its operating system.

Windows 2000 also provides two new print features: Internet printing and Active Directory support for searching for network printers. Internet printing allows you to submit print jobs to printers over the Internet and is covered in Chapter 6. For Windows 2000 Professional computers on a Windows NT Server Active Directory network, users can search the active directory for a network printer instead of having to type in the printer's location or browse the network in search of the printer. Available search criteria includes such things as whether the print device can print color documents or print at a specific resolution. If you are on a network without an active directory, then Windows 2000 offers the same browsing feature as Windows NT and Windows 98 in order to find your printer.

Searching for other Computers

Windows 98 and Windows NT allow you to search for a computer using its name on your local area network from the Find utility which you start by selecting Start, Find and then Computer. Windows 2000 Professional provides the same functionality.

Windows 2000 has renamed the term Find to Search. Otherwise the process of locating a computer is the same in Windows 2000 Professional.

Use the following procedure to search for a computer in using Windows 2000:

1. Select **Start**, **Search**, **For Files and Folder** and then select **Computers** in the Search for items section.

2. Next type the name of the computer you are looking for and click on **S**earch **Now**.

The results will appear in the Search results pane on the lower right portion of the Search results folder.

As with Windows 98 and Windows NT, you are presented with the computer's name, location and comment information. You can also double-click on the computer to access it assuming that you have the appropriate security permissions.

Mapping a Network Drive

Windows 2000 simplifies the mapping of network drives compared to Windows 98 and NT. Windows 98 and NT allow you to create network drive mappings from the pop-up menu of the My Computer icon and the Network Neighborhood and the Tools menu on Windows Explorer. Windows 2000 provides this feature from the same locations with the exception that you must use the My Network Places pop-up menu in place of the Network Neighborhood which is not provided by Windows 2000.

Like Windows 98 and NT, Windows 2000 assigns driver letters to disk drives, CD-ROMs and various removable storage devices. After assigning drive letters to any of these devices, Windows 2000 makes the remaining letters of the alphabet available for mapping to network drives. Mapping a network drive makes the drive act like a local hard disk and saves you the trouble of browsing the network looking for drives or folders that you frequently access. Mapping network drives also allows older software that was not designed to operate on a network to access network drives.

The Map Network drive dialog, shown in Figure 5.17 allows you to specify a drive letter and specify or browse for a network drive or folder in the same manner that Windows 98 and NT allows. It also provides the Reconnect at logon option.

The Windows 2000 Connect using a different user name option opens the Connect As dialog which is more intuitive than the Connect As option in Windows 98 and NT. The Create a shortcut to a Web folder or FTP site option opens the Add Network Place Wizard which steps you through the process of setting up a Network Place for either a Web folder or a FTP site as shown in Figure 5.18.

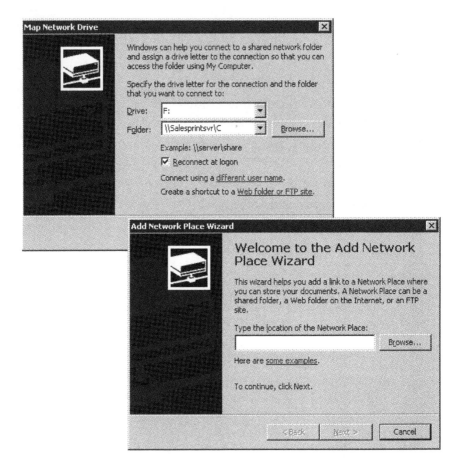

Figures 4.17—5.18 Show How to Map Network Drives, Web folders and FTP Sites

Once created, a icon representing the mapped drive appears in Windows Explorer and the My Computer Windows.

NOTE: *To remove a network drive select the Disconnect Network Drive option from the My Computer or Windows Explorer Tool menu or from the pop-up menu of the My Computer and My Network Places icons. Windows 2000 will display*

the Disconnect Network Drive dialog allowing you to select
and disconnect the mapping.

Sharing Local Resources

The sharing for folders and drives in Windows 2000 is very similar to how these resources are shared in Windows NT. The one exception is that Windows 2000 adds the ability to configure the share for offline access. Offline access configuration is new to Windows 98 users as well. The significant difference between Windows 98 and Windows 2000 is Windows 2000's ability to assign permission to individual users and groups, making a shared Windows 2000 folder or drive inherently more secure.

Sharing Folders and Drives

Windows 98 provides the following types of access to its shared folders and drives:

- Read only

- Full

- Depends on Password

Windows 98 provides for the assignment of a password for each of these types of access and expects that these passwords will be given network users who require access. The problem with this security model is that it does not allow the configuration of security for individual users and groups.

Like Windows NT, Windows 2000 allows you to create, manage and delete shares for a resource from the Shares property sheet on the resource's Properties dialog which you can access by right-clicking on a folder or drive and selecting the Sharing option of the resource's pop-up menu as shown in Figure 5.19.

Windows 2000 provides for the assignment of the following types of access to its shared folders and drives:

- Full Control

- Change

- Read

Like Windows NT, Windows 2000 allows you to delete a share with the Remove Share button or to create multiple instances of shares for the same folder or driver by clicking on the New Share button.

The Caching button displays the Cache Settings dialog as shown in Figure 5.20 where you can configure whether or not network users can create offline copies of the resources of its contents. The three available options are:

- Manual Caching for Documents

- Automatic Caching for Programs

- Automatic Caching for Documents

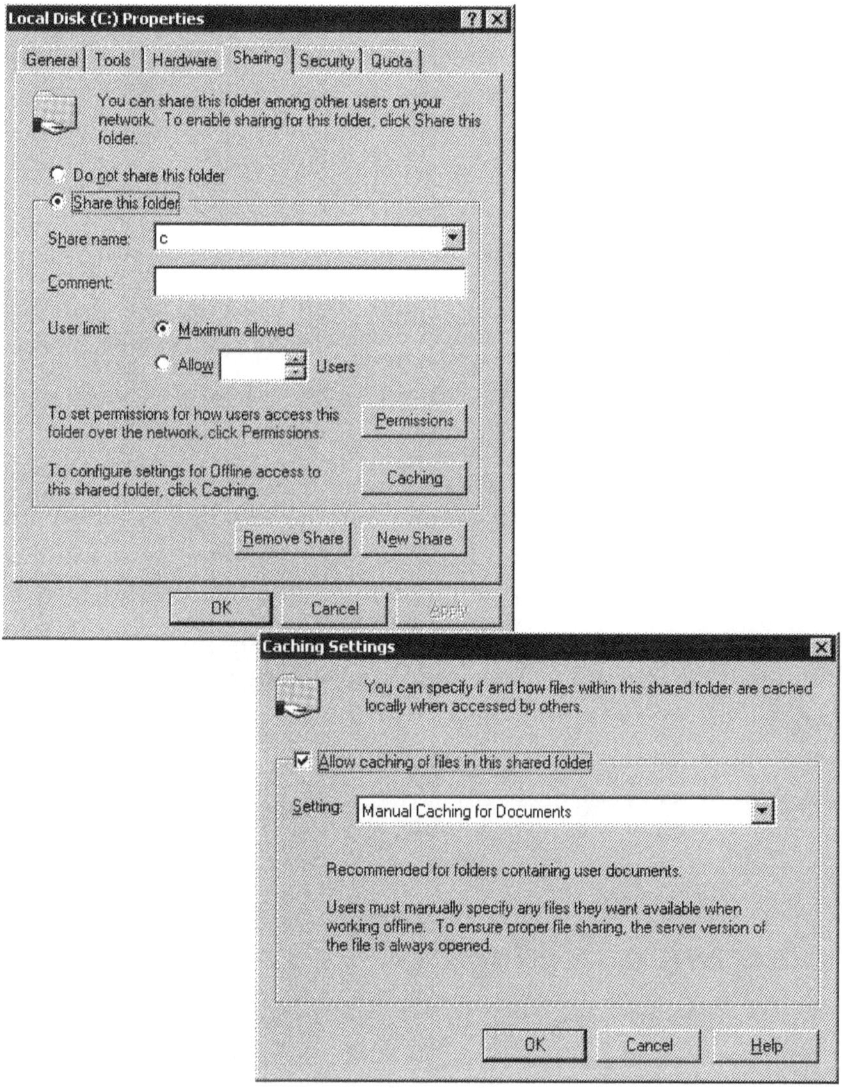

Figures 5.19—5.20 Show How to Create a Network Share and Establish Offline Access

NOTE: *Share level security is just one type of Windows 2000 security. If your drive is formatted with NTFS, you can also implement NTFS security and file encryption.*

Sharing Printers

Sharing a printer is basically the same for Windows 98, NT and 2000. However, there are a few small differences. Both Windows NT and 2000 have the ability to pre-load software drivers for other operating systems. This allows them to automatically download them to network computers which connect to the shared printer. Both Windows 2000 and Windows NT allow you to share a printer during its initial local installation whereas in Windows 98 you must first install the printer, and then go back to the Sharing properties sheet on the printer's properties dialog and share it.

You can also share your printer from the Sharing properties sheet on the Printer's Property dialog by selecting the Sharing option on the Printer menu on the Printer's print queue dialog or by right-clicking on the printer and selecting Sharing from the pop-up menu. Either way the printer's property dialog opens displaying its Sharing property sheet.

Sharing a Modem

Windows 2000 Professional has the ability to share a modem with other network computers and provide proxy services to remote networks such as the Internet thus allowing multiple network users to connect to the remote network simultaneously. A Windows 2000 Professional computer that has been set up to share its modem receives access requests from other computers on the local area network and forwards them on to the remote network and passes back any received data. Windows 98 and

Windows NT do not provide this capability but can act as network clients and take advantage of this service as long as they are set up to look for a DHCP server.

NOTE: *Windows NT applications, and some Windows 98 applica-
             tions may have to be configured in order to work with the
             shared network modem.*

NOTE: *Windows 98 Second Edition also provides this modem shar-
             ing capability.*

Modem sharing is enabled on the Internet Connection Sharing property sheet of the Dial-up Connection that will be used to establish the remote connection as shown in Figure 5.21. To establish a shared modem, select the Enable Internet Connection Sharing for this connection option. In the On-demand dialing section you can select Enable on-demand dialing to instruct Windows 2000 to automatically initiate a dial-up connection if one is not already open. This option ensures that network users will always be able to get access to the remote network.

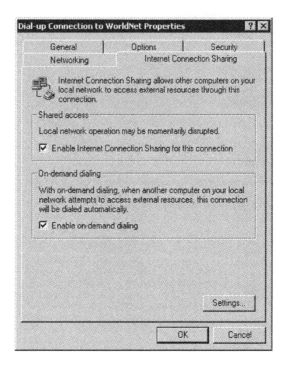

Figure 5.21 Establishing a Shared Modem

This feature is intended for implementation on small networks where Windows 2000 Professional's automatic IP addressing feature has been implemented. As soon as you enable modem sharing on your network, the Windows 2000 Professional computer with the shared modem establishes itself as a simple DHCP server. It then assigns itself a network address of 192.168.0.1 on a Class C network of 192.168.0.0. You will need to make sure that other network computers are set to look for a DHCP server. As these other DHCP enabled computers start up and log on to the network, the Windows 2000 Pro computer designated as 192.168.0.1 will assign them IP addresses in the range of 192.168.0.2—192.168.255.254 with a subnet mask of 255.255.255.0.

Chapter 6

The Internet

Getting Connected

A key component of the Windows 98 and Windows 2000 operating systems has been their integration with Internet Explorer. For years now Microsoft has been working to bring its operating systems and Internet Explorer together with the intention that the way you work and access the world wide web should be no different then the way you work with your desktop. By default Windows NT lacks this integration unless you install Internet Explorer version 4 or later. Out of the box, Windows 2000 provides Internet Explorer version 5.01, Windows NT provides Internet Explorer version 4 and Windows 98 provides Internet Explorer version 3. Of course, you can always install the most current version of Internet Explorer on any of these operating systems.

Internet Options

The Internet Options icon on the Windows 2000 Control Panel, shown in Figure 6.1, allows you to configure how you work with the Internet. It is very similar to the Internet Properties dialog on Windows 98. Both have the same set of property sheets and configure essentially the settings, although the Windows 2000 version is a little easier to work with. A Windows NT computer running Internet Explorer version 3, on the other hand, only allows you to configure a proxy server connection from the Internet icon in its Control Panel. Because of its lack of integration with Internet Explorer, the rest of your configuration must be completed from the Internet Explorer Options dialog.

Figure 6.1 Configuring Internet Options

The following list provides a brief overview of each of the property sheets on the Internet options dialog:

- **General**   Configure your default home page, the temporary storage of Internet files and the management of the Internet History folder

- **Security**   Create and manage a Web content zone of Internet sites and configure the appropriate level of security for each zone

- **Content**   Establish parental controls, manage certificates and configure how AutoComplete operations work

- **Connection**   Manage your dial-up connections, create new ones and configure modem proxy server access

- **Programs**   Specify which programs Windows uses for each Internet service such as your default e-mail application

- **Advanced**   Configure a multitude of settings that govern such things as multimedia, searching and security

NOTE: *You can also open the Internet Options dialog by clicking on Internet Options in the Tools menu of Internet Explorer. This has changed from Windows 98 where the Internet Options used to be located under the View menu in Internet Explorer.*

For more information on working with Internet Explorer version 5.01 refer to *Working with Internet Explorer* later in this chapter.

Finding a Proxy Modem Server

If your computer is on a network where a Windows 2000 or Windows 98 Second Edition computer has been setup to provide shared modem access to the Internet, you may want to use this proxy server as your connection to the Internet. The Windows 2000 Network Connection Wizard can help you make short work of this task.

Setting up a connection to the modem proxy server requires that your Windows 2000 computer's local area connection IP configuration be set up to look for a DHCP server as shown in Figure 6.2. As soon as you establish a connection to the modem proxy server, your Windows 2000 Professional computer will then request new IP configuration information. Your computer will release its previous IP address configuration and accept the new information sent to it by the proxy server. You will be leased an IP address on a Class C network in the range of 192.168.0.2— 192.168.255.254 with a subnet mask of 255.255.255.0 and a default gateway assignment of 192.168.0.1. The default gateway IP address is the IP address belonging to the modem proxy server. Anytime you are working with an application that requires Internet access, your computer will route all activity to the modem proxy server's IP address.

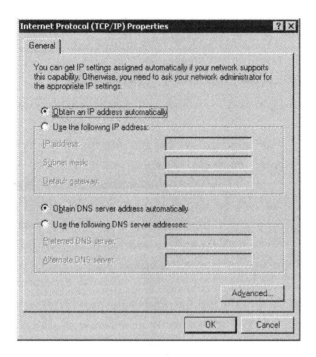

Figure 6.2 Configuring Your Computer to Look For a DHCP Server

To setup your computer to access to the shared modem:

1. Double-click on the Make New connection icon in the Network and Dial-Up Connections dialog to start the Network Connection Wizard and follow the instructions

2. When prompted select **Dial-up to the Internet**. The Internet connection Wizard will appear.

3. When prompted select **I want to set up my Internet connection manually** or **I want to connect through a local area network (LAN)**.

4. When prompted select **I connect through a local area network (LAN)**.

5. When prompted select the **Automatic discovery of proxy server** option and continue to follow the wizard's instructions

NOTE: *If for some reason your computer is unable to automatically locate the modem proxy server, try selecting Manual Proxy Server instead of the Automatic discovery of proxy server. You will then be prompted to enter the IP address of the modem proxy server and will be given the chance to exclude any Internet addresses for which you do not want to use the modem proxy server to access.*

Once established your interaction with the Internet should work exactly the same as if you were directly dialed-in with a local modem.

Working with Internet Explorer 5.01

Windows 2000 Professional introduces Internet Explorer version 5. The first thing that Windows 98 and Windows NT users who are used to working with Internet Explorer version 4 will notice is that very little seems to have changed. One thing that is missing in Internet Explorer 5 is the Channels bar which has been replaced with a new functionality in Favorites. Except for this everything else is where you would expect it to be.

However, despite their similar appearance, there are many differences between Internet Explorer Version 4 and 5. Some of the more important differences are listed below:

1. Microsoft has integrated the Windows 2000 Search feature into Internet Explorer as shown in Figure 6.3

2. Microsoft has added add and organize options to the Favorites bar making it easier to manage

3. The History bar now includes multiple views including: By date, By sire, By most visited and By order visited today

4. Microsoft has added a Go button on the Address Bar to make navigating the Internet more intuitive for new users

5. Offline web page support has been added

6. Error messages have been improved to provide more English-like information with suggestions for fixing many problems

7. A Folders Explorer bar has been added making it easy to jump from the Internet to a view of your local computer and network

Figure 6.3 Searching the Internet

Accessing the World Wide Web from Windows Explorer

Windows Explorer is a tool familiar to Windows 98 and Windows NT users. Windows 2000 has made several improvements to this utility which make it more useful for working with the Internet.

Windows NT's version of Windows Explorer does not provide any means for working with the Internet and is restricted to the local file system and local area network access. In Windows 98 Windows Explorer has been expanded to include the ability to access the Internet from the Address line, to access web sites stored in Favorites, to display a Links toolbar, and to include the addition of the Search, Favorites, History and Channels Explorer Bars.

Windows 2000 has improved upon Windows Explorer by adding the following list of new Features:

1. The modification of the address bar to include the Go button

2. The addition of the Search button on the Standard buttons toolbar allowing fast access to Internet searches

3. The addition of the History button on the Standard button toolbar making it easy to revisit previously visited web sites

4. The addition of the Folders button on the Standard buttons toolbar making it easy to swap back to a traditional view of Windows explorer

5. The migration of functionality from the Channels Explorer Bar into Favorites

Windows Update

Windows 98 introduced the Windows Update feature which allows a user to connect to the Windows Update web site for Windows 98 and automatically download and install the latest fixes, drivers, patches, service packs and enhancements for Windows 98. Windows 2000 Professional provides this feature as well.

Once you start the Windows Update process, your computer connects to Windows 2000 update site and receives a list of software updates, drivers, service packs, fixes and utilities that have not been installed on your computer.

NOTE: *In case you are worried about your privacy, don't be. Microsoft does not permanently collect and store any information about your computer.*

To activate the Windows update process:

1. Click on **Start**, and then **Windows Update**.

2. Internet Explorer starts and connects to the Windows 2000 Update web site as shown in Figure 6.4.

3. Click on **PRODUCT UPDATES**.

4. The first time you use the Windows Update feature you are prompted to install Microsoft Active Setup. Select **Yes** to continue.

5. A list of updates applicable to your computer's configuration appears as shown in Figure 6.5. Select a specific

6. update and click on the **Download** button. You will be prompted for confirmation.

7. Click on **Start Download** to download and automatically install the update.

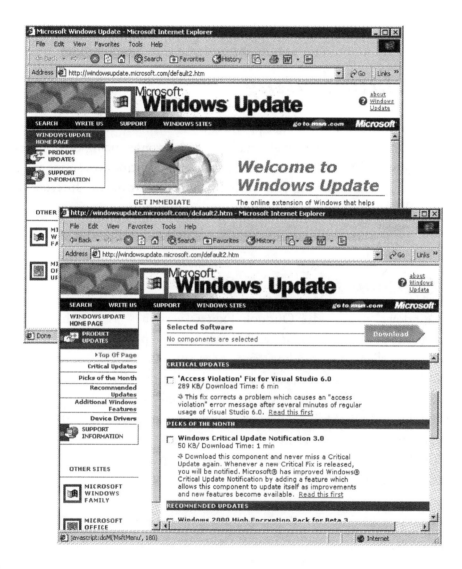

Figures 6.4 and 6.5 Demonstrate the Process of Applying Updates From the Microsoft Windows Update Web Site

Some updates require you to accept a license agreement or restart your computer after the update process completes.

Communicating

Windows 2000 Professional provides an assortment of Internet communication tools that provide e-mail and video conferencing capabilities all integrated with the Address book. In addition it introduces support for Internet Printing, allowing you to submit print jobs over the Internet to remote Windows 2000 print servers.

Outlook Express 5.01

Windows 98 provides Outlook Express version 4 as its e-mail and newsgroup application. Windows NT Workstation provides the Microsoft Exchange client for sending and receiving e-mail. However, most Windows NT users have probably installed Internet Explorer 4 or later which automatically replaces the Exchange client with Outlook Express. Windows 2000 Professional provides Outlook Express version 5.01 which also includes Windows Address Book version 5.01.

Outlook Express version 5 improves on the previous version in many ways, including:

1. When sending e-mail to other Outlook Express version 5.01 users, you can request verification of receipt as shown in Figure 6.6.

2. A dozen new stationary designs have been added along with a Stationary Setup Wizard which can be started by selecting Apply Stationary from the Format menu, selecting More Stationary and clicking on Create New as shown in Figure 6.7.

3. Support for multiple signatures has been added and is managed by selecting Options from the Tools menu and selecting the Signatures tab as shown in Figure 6.8.

4. You can now manage your Hotmail account Inbox and folders and even synchronize your contacts between Hotmail and the Address Book. Outlook Express will even help you set up a Hotmail account. Simply select the Account option on the Tools menu and click on Add and follow the instructions.

5. Support has been added for establishing multiple user identities. This permits people who share the same computer to create an identity which allows them to see their own mail and contacts when they log on and to apply a password to prevent others from seeing them. To create a new identity select Switch Identify from the File menu and select Manage Identities.

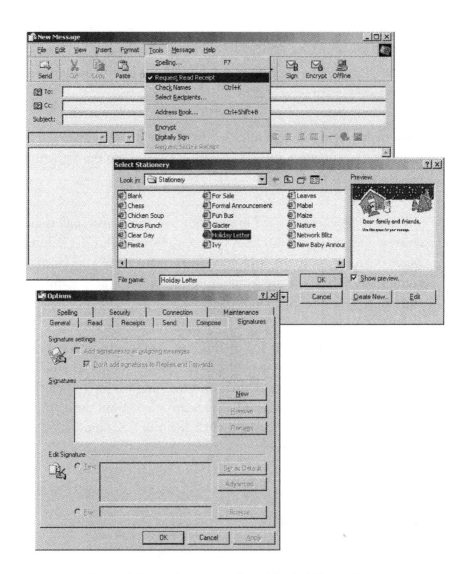

Figures 6.6—6.8 Demonstrate Several Outlook Express Features

Address Book

The Windows Address Book is a utility for storing all your personal contact information as shown in Figure 6.9. While typically thought of as a sub-utility of Outlook Express, Address Book is also a stand alone tool that integrates well with multiple Windows applications.

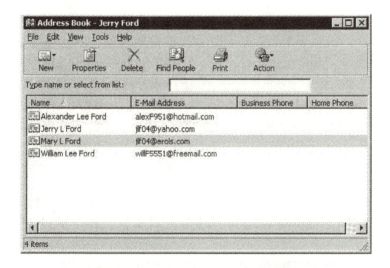

Figure 6.9 The Windows 2000 Address Book

Windows 98 and Windows NT users with Outlook Express 4 and Address Book 4 will notice very little difference with Address Book 5.01.

One new feature in Address Book 5.01 is the ability to create multiple identities. You can create an identity for every user of the computer. This allows each user to create and manage their own contacts and to password protect them so that other users cannot access them.

You can create new identities from Switch Identities option on the File menu of Outlook Express.

NOTE: *Even though the Address Book supports identities, you cannot create them from the Address Book unless you open it from the Start menu by selecting Start, Programs, Accessories and then Address Book.*

Another new feature in the Address Book is the ability to share your address book with other users. This feature complements the use of identities. To share your contacts with other users, simply place them in a shared folder.

As with Address Book 4, Address Book 5 supports integration with NetMeeting. This means you can establish conference calls from the Address book. This is done by selecting Internet Call from the Action button on the Address Book toolbar. The Address book is also integrated with the Fax utility, and you can select dialing information from it when using the Send Fax Wizard.

A new feature for the Address Book is the integration with the Phone Dialer utility. To dial the phone number of a contact in you address book, select the contact and click on Dial on the Action button on the Address Book toolbar as shown in Figure 6.10.

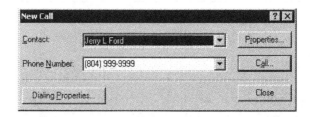

Figure 6.10 Dialing a Contact in the Address Book

Internet Printing

Internet Printing is a new feature introduced by Windows 2000. Windows 2000 Professional supports the ability to locate, install and print to remote printers over the Internet. The printer must be attached to Windows 2000 Server running Internet Information Server or a Windows 2000 Professional computer running Peer Web Services.

NOTE: *Internet printing is based on the new Internet Printing Protocol or IPP standard.*

You can connect to an Internet Printer by either providing its URL to the Add Printer Wizard. You can also find it with your web browser by typing its URL. Once you have located the Internet printer, you can install it. Installation may include automatically downloading the appropriate printer driver if the Internet printer has made it available. After installation you can submit print jobs to it and view its print queue via your web browser.

By connecting to the printer's URL address you can perform the following types of actions:

*   See the print jobs currently in the print queue
*   Examine printer properties
*   Pause, resume and cancel your own print jobs
*   Manage printer permissions and control all print jobs if you have the appropriate administrative permissions over the printer

TIP!   *If you are not comfortable working with the Internet printer with a web interface you can still work with the Internet printer the normal way. A icon representing your printer is automatically added to the Printers folder during its setup and you can manage your print jobs from there just as you would for a local area network printer.*

To connect to a Internet printer via its URL start the Add Print Wizard and click on <u>N</u>ext. When prompted select N<u>e</u>twork Printer and click on <u>N</u>ext. Select <u>C</u>onnect to a printer on the Internet or on your intranet and type the printer URL in the format of http://*printservername*/Printers/*share-name*/.printer as shown in Figure 6.11. Click on <u>N</u>ext and follow the remaining instructions.

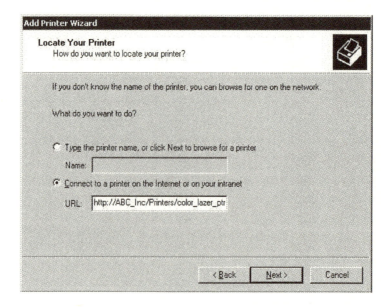

Figure 6.11 Connecting to an Internet Printer

NOTE: *You can also connect to an Internet printer from Internet Explorer by typing the following command http://PrintServerName/printers. This will produce a list of printers provided by the Internet print server. Select the printer you want and click on Connect under Printer Options.*

NetMeeting

NetMeeting is a communications tool that provides users with access to conferencing over the Internet. NetMeeting allows you to make phone calls over the Internet, set up conferences, share applications, share files, use audio and video and share a white board. A chat feature is included that is encrypted to ensure that your communications are secure. You use NetMeeting by joining a directory service that host your communications sessions.

Windows NT Workstation does not provide NetMeeting but it can be downloaded and added for free from the Internet. Windows 98 ships with NetMeeting version 2.1. Windows 2000 Profession provides NetMeeting version 3.01 as shown in Figure 6.12.

Among the improvements featured in NetMeeting 3.01 are:

- Data can be encrypted to ensure security

- Meetings can be password protected

- Shared programs open in their own windows making it easier to distinguish them from local applications

- Remote Control of remote user's desktops allows you to view and work on remote computers without having to physically visit them

Just as with NetMeeting 2.1, the first time you use NetMeeting 3.1 you are prompted to provide configuration information as shown in Figure 6.13. You will then be stepped through the process of providing required configuration information. You are prompted for your name and e-mail address, to select a directory that will host your NetMeeting sessions, to select your connection speed and to test your computer's audio capabilities.

One difference in installing NetMeeting 3.1 is that you can specify during initial configuration whether you want your name to appear in the directory list of the hosting directory service, instead of having to go back and configure from the Options option on the Tools menu.

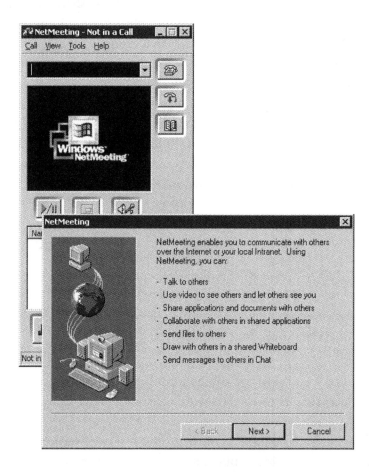

Figures 6.12 and 6.13 Show How to Configure NetMeeting

Glossary

Active Desktop. A feature of Windows 2000 that allows you to place live web content directly on your desktop which is automatically updated as long as access to the Internet is available.

AutoComplete. A feature added to Windows dialogs which attempts to complete fields based on the text that you have typed so far.

AutoCorrect. Automatically corrects typographical errors as you type in Windows dialogs.

Automatic IP Address. The ability of a Windows 2000 computer to either automatically assign its own IP address or receive one from a DHCP server.

Automatic Proxy Configuration. The ability of a Windows 2000 computer to automatically discover and configure itself to use a network proxy server in order to gain access to the Internet.

Client for Microsoft Networks. A piece of software which enables Windows 2000 Professional to participate as a client on a Windows network.

Computer Name. A name assigned to every Windows computer. If the computer is attached to a network its name must be unique.

Disk Quotas. The ability to establish a predetermined limit on the amount of space that users can consume on a local disk drive.

Domain. An organizational construct used by large Microsoft Windows networks for grouping, managing and securing computer resources on a network.

Encrypted File System. Adds additional security to Windows 2000 computers by providing for the storage of encrypted information on drives, folders and files on NTFS formatted drives.

FAT. A non-secure 16-bit file system that is supported by all Microsoft operating systems.

FAT32. A non-secure 32-bit file system introduced by Windows 98 but supported on Windows 2000.

Hardware Compatibility List (HCL). A list maintained by Microsoft at their web site that identifies all hardware which has been tested on Windows 2000.

Hibernation. The ability to save your current working environment before powering down a Windows 2000 computer and have it automatically restored upon startup.

Indexing. A Windows 2000 feature that allows it to build a searchable index based on the properties and contents of files located on local and network drives.

Internet Printing. The ability to submit print jobs to Windows 2000 print server via a connection to the Internet.

Local Area Connection. A connection to a local area network which Windows 2000 automatically creates when it discovers an installed network interface card. These connections are stored on the Network and Dial-up Connections folder.

Microsoft Management Consoles (MMC). A framework tool that contains management tools known as snap-ins from which you can administer your computer.

Modem Sharing. The ability of Windows 2000 to provide shared access to other network computers to the Internet or other external networks. The computer which provides this service is also known as a proxy server.

My Computer. An icon on the Windows 2000 desktop that provides access to local drives and the Windows 2000 professional Control Panel.

My Documents. An icon on the Windows 2000 desktop that provides access to a special folder where you can store all your personal files. A unique My Documents folder is created for each user of the computer and is only accessible by that user.

My Network Places. An icon on the Windows 2000 desktop that provides access to all network resources to which your computer is connected.

My Pictures. An icon on the Windows 2000 desktop that provides access to a special folder located inside you're my Documents folder where you can store all of your graphic files and view them without having to open them.

Network Connection Wizard. A wizard that steps you through the process of establishing connections to every available type of network connection. It is started by double clicking on the Make new Connection icon in the Network and Dial-up Connections folder.

Network Drive. A disk drive or folder located on another network computer for which a drive mapping has been created allowing the remote resource to appear as if it were a local resource.

Network Place. A link to a network drive, web folder or FTP folder which is stored in the My Network Places folder.

New Technology File System (NTFS). A secure file system supported only by Windows NT and Windows 2000 operating systems which features support for advanced features such as NTFS security and encryption.

Offline Files and Folders. A feature of Windows 2000 which allows you to view copies of network files when not connected to the network by storing copies of them on the local hard drive. Windows automatically resynchronizes your copies of these files with their network counterpart when you reconnect to the network.

Peer to Peer. A network consisting of 2 to 20 computers in which there is no centralized security or administration and where each computer maintains its own security account database.

Personalized Menus. A Windows 2000 feature which allows the operating system to adjust the Start Menu to the way your work by only displaying menu entries for the applications you use most often and hiding those which you seldom access.

Plug and Play. A feature which allows Windows 2000 to automatically detect, configure and manage peripheral devices.

Power Management. The ability of Windows 2000 to take control of your computer power consumption and adjust it based on current activity.

Print Pools. The ability to configure Windows 2000 as a print server and to create one logical printer from using two print devices which use the same print driver. Windows 2000 submits print jobs to the first available print device in the pool.

Print Priority. The ability to create multiple logical instances of the same physical printer and assign a different priority to each instance. Print jobs submitted to the instance with the highest priority are printed first.

Proxy Modem Server. A computer that has been setup to provide access to a remote network to other computers via its modem.

Safe Mode. A special startup mode used to troubleshoot computer problems during startup. It is activated by pressing the F8 key during startup.

Scheduled Tasks. A Windows 2000 feature which allows you to create a scheduled task using the Scheduled Task Wizard which runs according to the schedule that you define. These tasks are stored in the Scheduled task folder.

Service. A Windows 2000 component which provides a specific function for other Windows 2000 services and utilities.

Snap-in. A management application that runs within a Microsoft Management Console. It provides the ability to manage a specific Windows 2000 component or feature.

Stand by. The ability of Windows to save your current working environment in memory placing your computer into a low power consumption state. The computer is automatically returned to its previous state when the user presses any key or clicks on the mouse.

Synchronize. The process of reconciling the offline files with their network counterparts.

Taskbar. A component on the Windows 2000 desktop which contains the Start Menu, System Tray, various toolbars and icons for active applications.

TCP/IP. The default network protocol used by Windows 2000 networks. It is also the protocol required for communicating over the Internet.

Thumbnail Views. The ability to display a miniature view of graphic files in Windows folders allowing you to view them without opening them.

Toolbar. A feature found on Windows applications, folders and utilities which provides single click access to a commonly used command or feature.

Upgrade Packs. A special software program provided by application vendors that once installed enable earlier versions of their software to work properly on Windows 2000.

Workgroup. An organizational construct employed on Windows peer to peer networks that allows computers to be grouped into logical collections.

Index

A

U

V

W

About the Author

Jerry Lee Ford, Jr. is an author, educator and IT professional with over 12 years experience in the information technology field. He holds a Masters in Business Administration from Virginia Commonwealth University in Richmond, Virginia. Jerry is a Microsoft Certified Systems Engineer and the author of *Practical Microsoft Windows Peer Networking*. He has over five years experience as an adjunct instructor teaching networking courses in Information Technology. He lives in Hanover, Virginia with his wife, Mary, and their sons, Alexander and William.

www.ingramcontent.com/pod-product-compliance
Lightning Source LLC
Chambersburg PA
CBHW051236050326
40689CB00007B/947

There's more to building databases than just knowing SQL. Database design is the art of translating real-world requirements into an information model that can be implemented with a relational database. Which particular database product you use is not important. The concepts are the same.

This book presents a step-by-step guide to building a database. Topics include:

- Requirements gathering
- Introduction to SQL
- The model sequence
- Entities, relationships, and attributes
- Keys and indexes
- Entity-Relationship Diagrams
- Naming
- Normalization
- Implementation
- Breaking the rules

The author has been building databases for 28 years. He has developed systems for manufacturing, marketing, merchandising, medical, and military organizations, as an employee and as a consultant. He lives in Michigan with his daughter, five computers, and three printers.

ISBN 978-1-4357-3338-1